6.6

from Alex, Brett, Astrid

Love

Я

Я

LOVE OF MIRRORS

GARY HYLAND

INTRODUCTION BY LORNA CROZIER

Edited by Amy Caughlin.
Book and cover design by Duncan Campbell.

Cover image: René Magritte, *Portrait d'Edward James (La Reproduction Interdite)*,
1937, oil on canvas, 15 x 65 cm, Boymans-van Beuningen Museum,
© Estate of René Magritte / SODRAC (2007)

Printed and bound in Canada at Friesens.

Library and Archives Canada Cataloguing in Publication

Hyland, Gary, 1940-
Love of mirrors / Gary Hyland ; introduction by Lorna Crozier.

Poems.
Includes index.
ISBN 978-1-55050-391-3

I. Title.
PS8565.Y53L69 2008   C811'.54   C2008-900243-1

10 9 8 7 6 5 4 3 2 1

2517 Victoria Ave.
Regina, Saskatchewan
Canada S4P 0T2

AVAILABLE IN CANADA & THE US FROM
Fitzhenry & Whiteside
195 Allstate Parkway
Markham, ON, Canada, L3R 4T8

The publisher gratefully acknowledges the financial assistance of the Saskatchewan
Arts Board, the Canada Council for the Arts, the Government of Canada through the
Book Publishing Industry Development Program (BPIDP), Association for the Export of
Canadian Books, and the City of Regina Arts Commission, for its publishing program.

for Sharon Nichvalodoff

From her I drew again the power of sight,
and looked up, and I saw myself translated,
with her alone, to the next estate of light.

— DANTE, PARADISO, CANTO XIV, 82–84

CONTENTS

HAMMEL

MYSTERIES OF EVERYDAY LIFE

CHILD RUNNING

THE GREEN BOOK

EVENING LAUNCH

EDITOR'S NOTE

I never met Al Purdy so it is a rather odd that I should credit him with being the catalyst for a creative collaboration. It is even more incredible that he was able to accomplish such a task when he had already been dead for a year. In April 2001, I received a communication from Gary Hyland. He had been doing research for a tribute to Al Purdy and had stumbled across my Web site. In addition to my dedication to Purdy's work, Gary had noted my own poetry and had seen in it something he has never been able to ignore: an opportunity to teach.

Thus began a literary partnership that has certainly been a major influence for me. There is a Taoist saying: "When the student is ready the teacher will appear." Certainly, that was the case for me, and I imagine I am only one of many that Gary has graced and enriched with his distinct brand of literary mentorship. I learned to put aside the tentative questioning of the student and apply a more confident critical eye. I learned to trust my instincts. In short, I made the transition from someone who writes poetry to a living, thinking poet.

In time, what began as an apprenticeship evolved into a more equal exchange of both ideas and poetry. I read early drafts and suggested revisions to many of the poems that later appeared in *The Work of Snow* and *Hands Reaching in Water*. In some cases, the poems were even the result of poetic challenges we had set for each other, or philosophical debates that had spanned many conversations. I am still haunted by the ghosts of the many voices and stories that did not see publication.

When Gary began considering a collection of selected works, he asked me if I would go through his books and pick the "top ten" poems in each. It was a delightful task. I have always found the narrative style of Gary's poetry particularly engaging, and the music of his language often has me reading aloud to get the full flavour of the internal rhythm that enriches so much of his work.

As decision making for the collection began in earnest, we refined the selection process further. Each of us assigned points to the poems and then rated them based on our combined score. Overall, we had a very high level of agreement and when we disagreed the debates were good-natured and of short duration.

All the effort that went into the selection process did not prepare me for the impact of these poems organized into the final manuscript. Despite the familiarity I now feel for each, I was moved beyond words by the strength these poems have when they stand together. I hope readers of this collection will find not just Gary's story but, as is true in the best art, their own as well.

– Amy Caughlin

INTRODUCTION
The Ache Of Poetry

Poetry matters. Whole books have been written about why. The best argument for its necessity comes from a collection like this one. Gary Hyland, whom I claim as a friend, has been – it seems like forever – a crucial figure in Saskatchewan's enviable community of writers. Brought to poetry by the tragedies and beauty of the place he's from, Gary has crafted a body of work to be carried close to the heart through all the stages of a life. I can think of no one who has seen so clearly what is around him – people, land, city streets, stories in magazines or the local paper – and transformed them with such purity into the love and ache of poetry. From his home in Moose Jaw, he has "on a lone wing... / soared into the mind of the universe."

With wit and inventiveness, he populates his pages with kids bearing nicknames like Deke, Scrawny, Zip and Bumper. They spin on bicycle wheels from the real streets of his boyhood into his poems, but they've been altered with a storyteller's flair. They've been given breath and substance in the hands of a writer who can make myths out of the ordinary and the lost. Gary's characters are kids from any neighbourhood, yet they remain peculiarly local; Deke, for instance, dreams of flying over Moose Jaw like a contemporary Icarus, wearing wings stuck on his shoulder blades with Juicy Fruit gum.

Although many of the poems are humorous, they are achingly so. The comedy is flavoured with sadness, and sometimes bitterness, like the seed at the core of a jawbreaker. For Deke's graduation his mom gives him an ill-fitting neighbour's suit she has bought with her tips; Scrawny's mom, when he's four or five, runs off with an auctioneer, and Scrawny shoves the bike she buys him under a mainline freight. Outsiders in a middle-class world, they and their friends pose, bluster, fall in love with girls and sense a familiarity of spirit in the outcast Neesh, who lives in a shack by the CN line. No other poet I know shows such an affinity for the small, enormous pains suffered in a childhood stained by poverty. No one else endows boys like these with such a fierce and enduring grace.

One of Gary's gifts is his ear. He *hears* speech and transcribes it into a score on the page. Here's Deke talking about Dante's *Divine Comedy*:

> Worse yet it's ten thousand years old
> so you can imagine me in grade nine
> squinting at sixteen miles of poetry
> but I decided I was gonna get some laughs
> from this thing come hell or my old lady
> which is what does come – a trip to hell
> and jezzusmurphyman was it sumthin awful
> about as funny as your average math class.

Gary is, of course, writing in the form called the dramatic monologue, perfected in the Victorian age by Robert Browning and carried forward brilliantly by Eliot in poems like "The Love Song of J. Alfred Prufrock" and by Edgar Lee Masters in *The Spoon River Anthology*. A learned heir of that form, Gary is one of its most stunning contemporary practitioners. You can hear his ability to shift in and out of different voices with tonal precision in his series about a boxer who has taken one too many punches. In the book *After Atlantis,* the poet tells the story from the points of view of the boxer's manager, trainer, doctor and opponent, until finally we get the story from Vern, the boxer himself. No one can read Vern's take on the fight without being moved in the way that only poetry can move you. Vern says about his manager, "I wuz okay once...Arnie says." He goes on:

> Arnie...he's good
> a pal. He let's me do things
> when no guys are there –

punch onea the bags or...
or, y'know, dance kinda
inna ring
    sorta fightin
an I don't haveta pay
or clean up
    or pay money

The last stanza shows Gary at his best, stating what is literal and believable in the speaker's voice, but at the same time, striking the deep chord of metaphor:

So who knows he sez
maybe you'll come back
an I sez *from where*
an we always laff.

I've taught these poems for years at the University of Victoria; the silence in the room after students hear them for the first time is the silence of respect and sadness. How did he do this, my students ask, in such a simple poem?

If the mastery of the colloquial and the voicing of the lost were all that Gary had to give us, it would be enough. But he is a smart, curious and richly imaginative man who reflects on the last sermon of the 14th Dalai Lama, the mathematics of John Nash, Leroi-Gourhan's insights into Paleolithic cave drawings, the movements of tai chi, the burning of a child in Vietnam, the mirror of Elvis Presley. The scope and intelligence of his reading illuminate these pages and show up as well in his panegryrics to poets whom he admires: Pablo Neruda, Al Purdy, Anne Szumigalski, Patrick Lane, P.K. Page, John Hicks, Gwendolyn MacEwen, to name a few. Readers further see his erudition in his mastery of traditional forms: sonnets, pantoums, a glosa, dramatic monologues and epigraphs provide a rich countermeasure to the free-verse vernacular and open-form, lyrical meditations he excels at.

But perhaps what impresses me the most is the deepening wisdom, longing and lament that thread through this collection. The longing was there from the start; in an early poem, even the boy Deke was able to express it. Commenting on a girl who loved Hank Williams in a time of rock and roll, he says, "but you believed everything so beautifully / I used to wish you'd be right just once." Longing turns to despair in the perfectly rendered "Out of Habit," a poem about the breakup of a marriage. The perspective smoothly shifts between the husband and the wife. Nothing could be more terrible than his outburst of anguish juxtaposed with her detachment and control:

> He pulls into a closed service station.
> Trying to expel the pain, coughing, crying, he
> doubles over, slams himself against the door.
> She lights a cigarette and takes a slow drag.
> He looks like one of those black and white
> films, the old ones where nothing much happens.

Towards the end of the book the insights are more predominant and somber, with enough grit and texture to carry a reader to another level of knowing and loss. Those of us who know and love Gary as well as his poetry also know that he is ill with ALS. Never one to give up or turn away from any difficulty even when he "smashes into God," he has been able to transcribe what is happening into the cadences and gristle of his written words. You hear a new kind of poignancy in lines like "Your mind not recognizing / your body," and "I / fret myself to sleep, and each / day learn to breathe again," and "It's never as late as you think / It's always later." Never has hope been so sweet, so hard-earned and so purely expressed as in the final section of "Arguments in the Garden of Prayer." It is a poem to break the heart:

> The first sounds will be the bottle rattle
> of the milkman and the chattering sparrows.
> You don't get up right away. You listen
> to your mother clatter in the kitchen,
> your father shaking out the paper.
>
> The endless sun spills through the window.
> You think of school. All your homework is
> ready and all correct. New clothes beckon
> in the closet. A playground of friends awaits.

Your father's voice, low and casual,
spreads warmth and your mother's voice responds.
One of them turns on the radio.

A voice declares eternal peace and welcomes
you to heaven. Stretching, you decide to rise

In "November Waltz," a poem addressed to his father and mother long after their deaths, the speaker confronts the problematic couple who created him:

Look what I've become, you who feared
the dream-lost lad would never learn to work.
Look what I've become, you who thought
I was too frail or foolish, you who thought
I'd wear a uniform in danger or in jail.

Have I got it, father, have I got it
right at last? And, mother,
may I have this last waltz?

Yes, we say, for his father and mother, and for ourselves. Yes, Gary, you got it right, over and over again in your life and in these poems. In the early morning, open this book, read the pages and see what you've become.

— *Lorna Crozier*

HOME STREET

HOME STREET

Equator of my youth
from which I explored
every latitude
north and south,
I still gauge distance
from your boulevards
especially when I fear
the man I have become
has strayed too far from
the boy who trembled here.

THE BOY WHO ENTERS ROOMS

He finds havens in their homes –
a parlour, a sun porch, a study –
while in their kitchens his mother,
talking and talking and talking,
cuts or sets or perms their hair.

Rooms of hardwood, high windows,
velvet drapes, candlesticks on brick
fireplaces, clocks ticking in dark
wood. Brass lamps with glass bowls.
No worn lino here, no empty beer bottles.

He browses their magazines:
Liberty, Vogue, Colliers
and makes up stories for the photos –
menace for women in hats,
combat for men in uniforms.

Tuesday is Mrs. Grace. He always
takes down the fat leather
book, nestles its weight in his lap,
and turns and turns gold-edged
pages of adventures.

Friday: the house with the piano.
He converts the insect things
on her sheet music into songs
and hums them slow or fast
to the pace he sets the metronome.

He reads the words on their records:
"I'm Always Chasing Rainbows,"
"A Garden in the Rain," "The Day
After Forever" and makes up perfect
tunes with the neatest rhymes.

Mrs. Bedford's oak study has
a typewriter he must not touch.
He types with one hand while
the other catches the keys,
palming words like secret

spells. His rooms while he is
in them. Too soon
                    mother would call.
On the bus he sits beside her
not talking, eyes closed, trying
to keep the rooms inside.

CENTAUR

When old men spat from the bridge
I was the palomino
alone on green hills.

My hooves thundered death away.

My nostrils bulged
with the wild scents
where the creek snaked
under the spans.

I was delirious
in white clover
and blue-eyed grass.

They aimed nicotined fingers
where I plunged
through the smartweed.

Sometimes they laughed –
a skinny galloping
blur of a kid.

It gave them something
to say to each other

as I ran needing no breath
up down between the hills,
ran with my mane like a plume
into the long afternoon.

JERSEY NUT EAST OF JAVA

1.
Sunning himself on the luxury deck, Willoughby-Smythe
is wrenched from repose in his deep-padded chair
by alarms and the shouting of crewmen.
He bustles to the bow to watch approaching slowly
from the north a mammoth rectangular mass,
all red and higher and wider than he can see.
I say, it's a monstrous bloody red iceberg,
he says. *No iceberg, that,* a crewman snorts,
not red, not with such straight-cut sides.
Whatever that is, mate, it's been manufactured!
Everywhere passengers are praying or panicking.
A few excitable souls in kilts leap overboard.
Then the captain's voice rings from the speakers:
– to be alarmed. We have a clearer view from here
and we have definitely identified the object
which poses no present threat to the ship.
We may, however, be delayed an hour or so
until it passes. What you see before you,
ladies and gentlemen, seems to be a rather large
candy bar, a variety called Crispy Crunch.

Just one of the many adventures
from Miss Lee's classroom map,
a William Neilson company special
that outglittered nature
by floating four chocolate bars
strategically
among the earth's drab hues,
a luscious torture to unroll
before ravenous kids.

2.
Four tugs draw a giant Jersey Milk
through the Bering Sea to Magadan.

Inhabitants cram the harbour to view
the American imperialist confection.

Before the bomb check, peasants break
the barricades, swarm onto the thing,
shred the paper and chip away chunks,
tubfuls for the comrades back in the mines...

3.
Miss Lee never heard of the mean pirate M
the one-eyed attacker of honest sea traders
or his famous encounter with Admiral Drake
who along with his crew stands transfixed and helpless
as the mastless slab in blue and white paper
sweeps alongside with *Malted Milk* on its prow.

M takes their loot, their weapons, their rations
and all ninety of them for ransom as well.
Blast, says Sir Francis to those in his section,
the Queen will not pay for knaves such as we.
We deserve our doom in the brig of this varlet.
Then up speaks one captive, a sailor named Hyland,
a modest young lad, with an affable smile,
Good Captain, I tell thee we must not despair.
This vessel we ride in, strange as it seems, sir,
is a candy of sorts, a tasty container,
over here, for example, I've nibbled a hole.
With good teeth and stout stomachs, we still can escape.
All night in the dark hold they gobble in shifts
till sick with exhaustion and surfeit of sugar
at dawn they –

> "Hyland! Hyland!
> On cloud nine again?
> Now tell me the exports
> of Darwin, Australia."

4.
But northeast of Darwin
in the great Coral Sea
Jersey Nut Island is active again
belching sweet lava
and hurling nut fragments
as the natives row madly –

Then the four o'clock bell and at last I'm as free
as Drake and his crew on the Chocolate Bar Sea.

SMALL RELIEF

Wearing laced-up moccasins, running
into the wind through snow Ron Morin
could huff two blocks up Duffield Street
and out onto the open prairie to the rim
of the valley before the pack caught him.

Too winded to howl, they slogged faster,
three or four of them, knocked him down
in a flurry of fists and kicks, his breath
and theirs swirling together in the cold,
the blood from his nose lacing the snow.

And I watched. Twelve years old,
huffing from the run, wanting to see
the punishment for being Ron Morin.
I watched. Pleased it wasn't me. I watched.

HER CHOICE

She will not leave the car.
Her sisters, her brothers, mommy
and daddy are in Auntie Lill's
drinking lemonade, their laughter
bulging out like big bowls
of light from the windows.

She is hot and she is thirsty
but she will not leave the cozy
aloneness with herself in the car
where all the shadows and all
the sounds can be hers and
no one can put them to bed
or sweep them up or break them.

She can lean out the window
or snuggle with Mr. Muffles
or sing her song into the radio.
She will not be wrong. She will
not be called second or last.
She will not wear this dress.

Mommy calls from the door.
Auntie calls from the window.

She will not leave the car
and go inside and some day talk
too loud serving cake and lemonade
just so people will like her.
She will not call someone in
to places where they get eaten up.

AFTER THE PARADE

The last march is echoing
off the CP station
the kids from the bands
swirling through sidewalk mobs
the cars snarling
at unlocked intersections
everyone ignoring
the feeble traffic lights
people jostling, bumpers nudging

In the centre of High and Main
like a Royal Theatre hero
Brucie appears
cowboy hat snugged around his ears
and under his non-chin
cap pistol jammed into his pants
face lost in a gigantic grin
Bruce, twenty? thirty? forty?
directing traffic

and everyone's obeying
not as a joke, not to humour him
but because he's out there
and dammit *he knows what he's doing*
his arms (the same that conducted
the Royal's soundtrack orchestras)
moving in eloquent semaphore
(one hand on hip, a dramatic grimace
finger wagging at transgressors)
the traffic slowly flowing again

We're all pulling for him
when Louis the cop strides over
salutes and assumes the post
Brucie removes his Stetson
and bows to our applause
his hat dusting the pavement
just like Hopalong Cassidy's

VACATIONS

Holidays we spent in places close and measured
because of the need to get home nights,
but that didn't make them any less treasured
than trips to the coast, mountains or northland sites.
We escaped to huts in woods that nuzzled the town
and sailed sticks in streams after summer rains.
We tightroped the tracks and liked to spit down
from the bridge onto passenger trains
while scouting for bottles – a penny apiece.
In rivers and railroads and stockyards we played
without leagues or lessons or the frustrations
of parents. Oh, now and then the police
would knuckle our doors, but no charges were laid
to curtail our glorious educations.

CONSEQUENCES

It is a summer after supper,
the stars just starting to form,
and Sharon Armour is the judge.
She has grade seven lore and we
are mere grade four or fives.

I wear the striped green T-shirt
that helps me pretend I am
a sailor on the river. Though Mrs.
Merrit's housecoat sways on
wire like a phantom chaperone,
we play Truth or Consequences.

When it's your turn you choose
to answer a question or suffer
a fate of short and long kisses
with a partner of the judge's whim,
a brief Morse code liaison
in the garden behind Merrit's garage.
I usually prefer Truth because
we river sailors have better
wishes than rubbing lips with
Sherry Merrit or Betty Ogden.

But this one's too risky, nothing
I dare answer. I try to disguise
my pleasure when the judgement,
five short and five long, is with
the judge herself, forerunner
of the older women of my desire,
tall, brown eyed, dark haired
in jeans and shiny penny loafers,
new breasts like strawberries
beneath her white sweater.

We huddle in the drooping grass
on the garden's edge, kiss in slow
tremors, and talk a bit between.
The stars surge with liquid light.
After eight she asks how many
and, as coolly as I can through
the spin and daze, I answer six.
During number twelve, moister,
more sustained, I hear a voice.
Not my mother, nor my brother
sent to spy and drag me home.

It is so familiar to me now.
This night it seems more urgent
with each shout, as if the caller
wants me home because he knows
all garden myths must fall to grief.

PINTSCH COMPRESSION COMPANY TOUR

I am ten when I follow my father along the narrow, ankle-deep rut
the workmen have worn in the weeds. Over a footbridge, through
the roundhouse thrumming with monstrous steam engines (greasy
men in grey caps staring), down the concrete steps into the squat
brick building that reeks of oil and gas. I scurry as he almost
disappears in the gloom. Grime is steamed on the windows. Floor,
walls, ceiling – black with soot. Dingy lamps smoulder in metal cages.
I am shown the storage tanks, compressor, pumps and valves, the
huge pipes that take gas through tunnels under the mainline tracks.
The giant hose with metal couplings that he plugs into the cars, or
the Pullmans don't work. So the fancy people can be served Cornish
game hens. So they can wear shirt sleeves as they tunnel through
winter. He wipes a gauge with a rag, explains the range of readings,
shows me the logbook, the columns of smudged numbers. The
punch clock and cards. Seven years, never an absent shift.

I recall picnics cancelled, ball games missed, the fringe of beer bottles
around his chair. I want to be running with Tippy or drawing pictures
of my secret place. No, I haven't any questions. I follow him back to
the bridge, its timbers warm in the sunlight. He tells me I can make it
from there.

Years later, long after the funeral, with three sons of my own, I
understand and weep. Then I sit and write nine questions about
compressors, gauges, trains.

WALKING WITH SONS

Once they mastered walking there was a moment
that was magical. I'd hold out my hand
and without hesitation they would plant
theirs in mine, soft and small as a nestling.
I could lead them anywhere then. Into quicksand.
Into traffic. But, often, I'd let them lead me –
stooped, shuffling down walks and alleyways,
through stores, along the weedy river shore
while they explored spiders, candy wrappers,
strange stones, robins, bulldogs and pinball games.
They'd point and scurry and I'd skitter after
their trusty charge, dispensing facts and names.
Those walks were by far the best, improvised
from whims, me feigning, then filled with, wonder.

MICHAEL SKIPPING

Propelled by nothing
more secret than joy
for one heartbeat
my son clears the ground

As he skips and sings
there is an instant
if camera-caught
that would show him
touching nothing.
The perfect moment
for both of us –

Michael earth-loosed
by his own lightness
wonderfully unweighted
free of all reaching
and launched by fuel
of my refining.

MICHAELMARK

Your names become a collective noun – MichaelMark.
A three-year-old, a four-year-old in endless competition,
a crazy graph of making war and making up.

Each day calibrating what counts and what doesn't,
no better than the rest of us at separating the joys of triumph
and participation, but needing the other's opposition.

When you storm up in tears I explain: *Boys, you are one,*
like your hands, left and right, that can resist or assist
each other. See this hand is Mark, this Michael.
Now they push against each other and grow strong,
now they lift this chair together. That's how things get done.

Ah, sweet reason, paradigms of Logic 101 applied
to fraternal spats. In no time you are bored with wisdom
and roar away to devise another tussle, Michael yelling,
I'm the right hand. I'm the right.

THE FIRST MOON
OF MOOSE JAW

INTERPRETER

Neesh the Indian conserved words
let us puff rollies in his shack
near his creek by the CN line
dozing in his rocker
while we struck matches and poses
that might have burned us all –
tough guy preadolescents who later
scrubbed brown fingers with snow.

Ten years at least he was there
and was never once outside they say,
there were stories about what he ate
and how he got his tobacco.
In winter by the east window
in summer by the west he watched us
playing on the long cinder hills
by the tracks and on and in his creek.

Often I thought about old Neesh
whether he was wise or mad,
whether a whole tribe slept in him
awaiting a sign of war or peace.
From Sleigh Hill one night I watched
his shadow rocking and smoking
till a winter fog intervened
and I couldn't even see the shack.

Between us, beneath the darkness
and the fog, was his creek and
under the ice, Neesh had said, was water
just a bit, refusing to freeze,
keeping the mud moist, and in the mud
were seeds and creatures still alive.
Beneath such layers I imagined Neesh
and the rest of us, side by side.

WHAT YOU ARE DOING NOW

You are in grade twelve
and you and this poem
meet for the first time
in an English classroom
when you would rather be
almost anywhere else
gazing   lazing
dancing   snoozing
kissing cruising
but all of history
from Cro-Magnon clans
to Puritans
to the Department of Learning
was mobilized to get you
and this poem here/now

and you're thinking   *hey*
not so bad so far   *hey*
I understand most of this
At least it's not that gloopy
antique tombstone stuff/not

O spirit soft of summer's breezes
Who dwelleth in yon western reaches
Where gulls conspire to form friezes
With white waves on craggy beaches

at least it's not that snarly
strung-out lumpy stuff/not

      my snow

      stems

      roses

      till they

            (petal

          me)

Hey this is like football
He pins   *I boot*
Hey it's basketball
He passes   *I shoot*
Manoman I can do it!
Hey there's nothing to it!

Then your teacher announces
that you have forty minutes
to write an analysis
of this poem
           and when you look
the poem spits in your face
and stops

SCRAWNY'S NATURAL LOOK

The wind's a real drag
You get your hair just right
the wave angling off
scoops along the sides
the ducktail centred –
a shining construction
of Brylcreem and water
Then you step outside
Zap – instant hedgehog
Fifteen minutes combing
shot to ratshit

Winter's a better deal
Even in a blizzard
your hair freezes
into a helmet
Then you amble into the A
join some girls and sit there
looking natural
as you hair melts
and dribbles down your neck

NOT QUITE KINSEY

Magoo's the first to report
authentic back seat encounters
having dated Hot Pants Drake
off and on   *Mostly on, ha-ha*

His first car's a '49 Ford
and after only three days
a brassiere's slung from the aerial
a real roomy job, maybe 38C

He explains it's a trophy
of his first conquest in the car
and naturally we're impressed
Hey Magoo, that musta broke your wrist

Who was she – Gina Lollamaidenform
*You can get **busted** for flashin that*
But in a week it's no big deal
till one day we're parked at the A

Up comes Mrs. Magoo, his mother
short, fat, huffin like a steam engine
So that's where it went she hollers
She grabs a strap and yanks away

bending the aerial almost to the hood
I have this vision of his old lady
with a brassiere in her fist
zoomin over the city like Wonder Woman

But Magoo hops out and pulls it down
She jams it into her purse snarlin
Get straight home you little shit
and storms away down the street

Magoo sits red-faced for awhile
his head against the steerin wheel
then pops up, grins and says
Anyone else wanna date with my old lady?

HANK WILLIAMS WILL BE 56 TODAY

Jesus, Melody, for dumbness you were A plus
cookin up apple pies in your mum's kitchen
and goin on to me about that western fart
Listen, Deke, this one's called "Jambalaya"
while I'm thinkin he has nasal constipation
and spinnin Bill Haley and Little Richard.
You sayin he wasn't dead but in a clinic
for repairs and almost ready to rise again,
but you believed everything so beautifully
I used to wish you'd be right just once.

You believed there was no death in death
not for anyone you knew enough to care about.
George VI wasn't dead or James Dean or Bogart
and the kid from Westmount who got squashed
by the truck on Home Street still played
every winter on the road by your house.
You believed clouds were halos for the earth.

But then you got yourself a ramblin man
and a run-off daughter you couldn't dream back,
so I wonder if it all leaked out, your faith
and whether you kick puppies off your lawn
and smoke alone at night sipping lemon gin.
Or are you in Prince George or Peterborough
rolling a pie crust and singing "Jambalaya"?

THE FIRST MOON OF MOOSE JAW

We stash our clothes in Scrawny's car
and go bare-ballin down by the dam
me, Scrawny, Zip and Magoo
After, we dress in the back seat
Magoo, as usual, still in the creek
and the sun meltin the upholstery
A few horn blasts and he waddles up
sloshes over Zip and starts dryin
hunched-up like a pregnant walrus
Zip takes exception to being drowned
and they start shovin back and forth

Before long Zip pins Magoo's head
and somehow pushes the poor bugger
so his rump's jammed outa the window
till the bulgin flesh spills out
and sizzles on the hot chrome trim
Magoo screams and squirms first-rate
but Zip's got him pretzeled real snug
Scrawny he never misses a good chance
so he starts the Dodge and we light out
with a windowful of Magoo's pink cheeks
bouncin like a coupala baby pigs

Right away I see where we're headed
cause there's a mess of Holy Rollers
havin a prayer orgy down the road
There musta been maybe three hundred
fryin in their shiny Sunday outfits
around some thumper on an oil-drum stage

Then we roars up like Judgement Day
and Scrawny leans out and hollers
Behold, brothers, the face of Lucifer
He cuts through the field to give em
a close-up wide-angle view so to speak
then floors her and we dust outa there
horn ablastin and Magoo ascreamin
and us three roarin like all royal hell

THE DULLS

Eleven/eleven thirty
Zip and Scrawny have the dulls
lean on buildings/meters/cars
shoot blue smoke into the swirl
of moths around the lights

All day nothing has happened
nothing worth yawning for

No one to clock them home
as they smoke and wait

Lightning zips from nowhere
Thunder cracks across their faces
The world splits like an egg
down the street's white line

A huge forehead rises in the rift
eyes with webs of fireworks
head lifting/mouth opening
larger/blacker than any cavern

A voice rips through their hair
THE MAN WHO HATH NO MUSIC IN HIMSELF
HATH A SPIRIT DULL AS NIGHT

Zip stretches and yawns
Scrawny peers at the great head
Hey, Big Face, ya gotta light?
It passes a little time

PIRANHA SCHOOL

Immobile
except for gills
lifting in unison
we monitor subtle currents
sense elusive variations
in pressure

When Magoo
slants too far
for knowledge
our eyes pull him
thrashing
out of light

As he chokes
we strike
with sharp laughter
shred him in seconds

A cloud of blood
billows
in the aisle

DEKE AND DANTE

What happened was in our social text
the author says *The Divine Comedy* by Dante
is onea the best books of all time.
With that title I think its gotta be funny
so I tool on down to the library
and Mrs. Burns falls off her stool
when I ask for it but she gets it
and it looks okay, y'know nice and small
so I head home and open it.

                         Well shit
you never saw such goddamn small print.
Looked like the Lord's Prayer on a dime
with footnotes longer than the story
only it wasn't a regular-type story
but a jeezus poem which if it was printed
the right size would outweigh *The Bible.*
Worse yet it's ten thousand years old
so you can imagine me in grade nine
squinting at sixteen miles of poetry
but I decided I was gonna get some laughs
from this thing come hell or my old lady
which is what does come – a trip to hell
and jeezusmurphyman was it sumthin awful
about as funny as your average math class.

I won't lay the whole scene onya but Dante
gets outa hell and hits purgatory next
then heaven before swingin back to earth
and never a fraction of a joke anywhere
but I stuck her out because to tell the truth
I got so I kinda liked that snazzy lingo
and the sharp way Dante zapped these losers
he decided oughta be dumped in hell
even a coupla popes.

But most of all
there was this Beatrice babe he loved
who was right-out-of-this-world beautiful
and it was her that inspired and guided him
right up to God's goddamned front porch.
All the time I kept imaginin Beatrice
was Elaine Wells and I was this Dante guy
and I sailed through that whopper of a book
in I'd say only about two or three months.

DEKE OVER MOOSE JAW

I'd like to pull an Icarus
swoop outa here on wings
made of magazines, old exams
book reports, gobs of Juicy Fruit

Old Newman scribbling fast
(to avoid the sodden wads)
the wonders of ancient Greece
would hear glass break, turn

see me gone, the window broken
and lead the class to view
my mangled corpse three flights down
victim of an overdose of school

I'd hover long enough to laugh
buzz them once and head for sky
No need to fret of sea spray here
nor would the prairie sun

melt the grip of Wrigley's best
God, what a sight I'd be
looping loops with Bumper's pigeons
in the silver maze of aerials

I'd ride the sky for five years
and land when I was twenty-one
jitters gone, able at last
to handle gravity with grace

THE OLD LADIES

1.
The night Elaine dumped him
Deke performed with Fet
a Wayne and Shuster skit
that had the party roaring
then he ducked out early

His mother was sewing
his sister's wedding gown

He sat down beside her
the needle diving
into white satin

When she felt his head
on her shoulder
she stopped

set aside the dress
so it wouldn't get stained
and stroked his hair

2.
His mother's razor strap
raised burning welts
on Zip's arms and legs

When he came in from school
she'd snarl *I've got you now*
and whack and whack away

She listened to "Ma Perkins"
sipping coffee-cup gin
and sometimes fell asleep

One day she barrelled in
with her roundhouse best
the strap smacking his arm

He grabbed it by the neck
wrung it from her hand
and said *I've got **you** now*

She wept as he rolled it up
He still keeps it on a nail
in the corner of his basement

3.
Scrawny was four or five
when his mother ran off
with an auctioneer

He was buying
and she was selling
his father used to say

When he turned ten
she brought him a bike
then got lost for good

Two years later
he shoved it beneath
the mainline freight

4.
For graduation
Bumper got a watch
Zip a record player
Magoo a typewriter

Deke living on his own
ousted by his father's fists
got a neighbour's suit
purchased by his mother
for three months worth of tips

The lapel was too fat
the pants too baggy
but he wore it without a word

He sat in the front row
on the wide stage
blushing in the dumpy suit
No record player, no watch
but all she could afford
and he would wear it anywhere

She sat near the side aisle
in her sister's beige dress
shadows and rouge concealing
the other price she paid

DEKE LEAVING HOSPITAL

Each time Dad's heart nearly stops
they move him further from the earth
and after riding the elevator
I find him weaker, paler than before
his eyes scrubbed like winter air
his skin dry, cool as glass

On the bus afterwards
I remember his raging at Mom
especially the time in the kitchen
I was big enough to step between
how as he slouched away
he seemed to be descending stairs

Now I could lift him in my hands
and the fingers that bruised
perch like birds on my arms

If he's released again
he'll return fast enough
rising a floor or two
to make a smaller dent
on a wider mattress

One day they'll find he's out of floors
They'll set him on the gravelled roof
and from there he'll slowly rise
to the coldest corner of the sky

WALTƧ

SHANIDAR

*"...at least seven different kinds of flowers were laid in
a shallow Neanderthal pit in Shanidar, Iraq."*
— Jeremy Campbell, Grammatical Man

And she died
and I dressed her in her robe of dreams
and scraped a resting space from the hard land
and laid her in
and in her hands and in her hair placed seven flowers
         sparks of night   tickle-sneezes
         proud heads   everywheres
               hide-from-sights
         swan's throats   dusty suns
and she had worn them all
and brought them to our camp
and to my eyes sick of sand
and with their grow-agains I traced
her form
and then threw on the earth
and stayed the sky dark through
and watered them

IT COULD HAVE BEEN

He says things are "swell." She thinks
that's swell. He smokes, so she smokes.
He smokes Sportsman. She smokes Sweet
Caporal. He has no car so they walk
to movies, dances, restaurants
through the new park after supper.
They sit on the grass and smoke.
People going home late at night
see their cigarettes like fireflies
against the dark mounds of trees.

He is a hardware clerk, 28.
She is a beautician, 21.
He has those swell city moves mother
warned her about before they left
the homestead where she was born,
its roof rotting and starting to leak,
the chickens given to neighbours
for a promise of eggs. The cow
sold and slaughtered the same day.
Not a kernel of crop to fret about.

Her mother doesn't like his type.
Her sisters whisper rumours.
But she is deep down sure of him.
They've already talked of babies
and she has a list of names,
one of which is mine.

In their second summer, they wed
and now eight months later,
March frost scrawled on windows
a cold paw creeping across
the kitchen floor, the old bed's
metal frame rattles with the pulse
of my spawning and nothing else
because it's two bloody a.m.
and he is primed with liquor
and looking for a little and she's
just too rundown to resist.

And if it wasn't like that, well
given how things turned out,
it could have been. If it wasn't,
it damn well could have been.

And then they sit up and tug
sheets and blankets to their chins.
Both silent though thinking.
How come it isn't all that swell?

He lights a Sportsman. She lights
a Sweet Cap and they don't talk.

Just two dots of light in the dark
apartment, almost merging
once when they inhale together.

LAMENT FOR A LITERAL LOVER

"Make me a cage of tiger lily stripes," she said.

Twice he endured tirades from old ladies
who caught him in their garden after dark
A dog removed a section of his best jeans
and once he stepped through a hothouse pane
soaking his runner with blood
but he got his bag of tiger lily stripes
and a tube of Krazy Glue
and set out to build a cage
for the bird of his romantic paradise

He kept the stripes in an envelope
where first his mother found them
and took a pair to replace the eyebrows
she lost when the gas stove exploded
Then his son saw they looked like licorice
and promptly gobbled half a dozen
It was his wife burnt up the rest
for a useless bunch of tiger lily stripes

Disgraced he wept and wrote to her:
Due to the current shortage of building materials
I cannot construct the edifice you desire

To which, eventually, she replied:
O lovely fool, you read me wrong
not a real cage, not real stripes
and most, O most of all, not you.

DELUSIONS

The man who thinks his wife's a hat
has an extreme paranoiac syndrome
marked by the most bizarre delusions.
Weeks earlier, convinced she was
a dish of butter, he bruised her
trying to spread her on a muffin
(which of course was not a muffin
but the Sunday *New York Times*).
And while she was a Chev he nearly
drove her crazy checking her oil.
When she was a hat he merely wanted
to brush her off and hang her in the closet.

Meanwhile next door Roger just-wed
thinks his Lynn's an angel on a bun.
And Lori in the condo opposite
wakes beside a dashing knight of neon
even while his white horse, tethered
out front, shits upon her lawn.

MRS. BINNER'S GARDEN LORE

It was Brittany, a fishing village
See those are the masts beyond the walls
In the harbour of cod and halibut smells

Claudine and I stayed with Madame Noel
in this cottage here on the left
and here, right here, in the backyard
this was her garden, her pride
the only garden in the village

You cannot see for the high wall
the roses, marigolds and dahlias
that mocked the barren soil outside

(I had forgotten, indeed, forgotten entirely
until you found this photograph)

His name was Eugene Boisclair
and he came into the garden
on the name day of St. Therese
to buy flowers for his Therese
the daughter of a dairy farmer

He came through this door
a fisherman young and awkward
in his first courtship, shy as a finch
clutching the tinkling bell too late
to hide from Claudine and me

He bought the dahlias, I remember
Madame Noel's specialty, big as soup plates
nurtured near the outdoor privy
and while he waited we went into our act
rehearsed on other village lovers
I the beau, Claudine the belle, me
shoving dandelions in her face, she
all ablush and giggling like a goose
No, Eugene, I dare not take them
But why, Therese, my little cabbage
Dahlias give my cows dry teats

When you hear of someone's death
you think of when you saw them last
what thoughts of you they took to God

The night of our garden game
they found Eugene dead, hanging
from a beam in Therese's father's barn
the dahlias crushed inside his coat

Therese wept for three months I am told
and no doubt the fault must lie with her
One must know how to spurn a man

We were eight and nine and not to blame
You see, I had forgotten entirely

The village sat on mounds of sand
but love and care within the wall
made the soil as rich as chocolate
It was the only garden in the village

A VISION LOCATES HIM NEAR HER

She is at the fire while he stamps in the woods,
dream-flung beyond the safe halo of
her camp. She stares at flames, not higher
to where the leaves quench stars, never
looks around when he lurches and stumbles in
a brook. No fear. Not her, night-caught
in the woods. At every odd sound he searches
the dark, his dread one cause for standing near
her light. He can almost hear the spongy
tread of paws while she takes the long, nodding
way to peace. He will wait the night by her
in bark and moss upon a fallen birch
far from the warm repose of home. Soon dawn
will come, shy, wearing a bright nest of clouds.

OUT OF HABIT

They discuss things in the car driving
nowhere up and down the streets so that
if one of them screams or weeps the kids
won't be disturbed. The kids are at home
watching a Disney flick in the family room.
She is not sure how much she will tell him
whether to mention the other man or maybe
just the job having to keep her away.

He sits too erect, arms stiff, hands tight.
Tonight is different in a way he doesn't know.
What has happened? What is going on?
Everything he says begins with *but*.
It's raining. He can't find the wiper switch.

She wishes she'd brought some cigarettes. Now
that she has started she must finish the job.
Somewhere in this purse there are cigarettes.
His rational spiel is almost over. She
breathes deeply, mumbles that she doesn't want
to be married. She has no reasons. Just that.
There is no traffic, no one on the sidewalks.
She looks at house lights through wet glass.
How many of them she wonders, how many.

He pulls into a closed service station.
Trying to expel the pain, coughing, crying, he
doubles over, slams himself against the door.
She lights a cigarette and takes a slow drag.
He looks like one of those black and white
films, the old ones where nothing much happens.

He gets out, walks a while in the cool rain,
over and over slamming wet fist into wet palm.

Her breath mists the windows. He gets in,
turns on the defogger, the headlights, the wipers.
Out of habit the car returns them to the house.

THE EXQUISITE BEAST

At the casual hover of a hand
your skin converts to camouflage
and reflexively you arm yourself.

But the exquisite beast, the animal you fear
is dead, died years ago, wasted
from running, something bursting in his brain,
flesh and fur gone from his carcass, white bones
sinking in the ground-drift of time.

Your eyes have been lying all these years.
And the terrified others, the game safe
and love forfeit, have all been lying.

You stay on the plains away from trees
and ledges where he might pounce. All
through the night your cabin lights blaze.

But he is dead. He is dead. There is a path
you never take along the coulee's brow.
Follow it and find his ordinary bones.
Spend a night in conquest of them.
Then ride out of your badlands. Home.

WALTZ

The man who claims he does not dance alone
lies. Fingers on flesh confound his eyes.

Love is a lovely simulation,
the sham that dancers hear one song,
become synchronous souls ascending.

But those notes that move now in me
will never make this melody again
nor raise in you a matching strain.

And though you are beautiful (nowhere in Norway
are fjords the fragile blue of your eyes)
and though we could waltz your way and mine
in manifold symmetry, we stay as isolate
as stars. Between us, lifetimes of darkness,
caves of space, we the hermits burning time.

YUGEN

You are the saying of your name
and the silences before and after
your name is said. There is none
of these without the other and all
are the spell which happens to me
whenever your name

is spoken. Wild geese, like one wing,
vanish through clouds, reappear.
Geese, clouds, the pale spaces
between are the vision
I fall into as a brook enters
a stream when I hear

your name spoken I slide
into one of the ways you are in me
and move out and apart on a song
of longing as one who roams
unconcerned far into a forest
to receive the music at

its heart. Your name is you
awakening me deep in this
valley where the sun kindles hills
of cherry blossoms and their light
spills into my eyes and their scent
fills me.

TOO CLOSE THE MOON

The summer of his mother's death
the wind-combed valley
was full of soothing women's
voices, one poet's lilting above
the rest, and the lake, long and blue
with sky, edged green with poplar leaves.
He and the poet walked from the hills
into waves of durum, the sun
so bright they wept.

Too close the moon at night –
the window white with it,
cool, thinner than frost, while he
burned with memories,
sheets spilled on the floor.

His skin so alive he felt
the graze of blood,
the trace of aspen leaves.
It must have been his mother's
skin, its histories of pain.

The valley echoed at night –
frogs, coyotes, voices over the lake.

Days full of words.
The poet's like plovers,
sure-winged, singing
in flight. Her mouth ardent
on the land, and on his
mouth, all on the edge
of another season.

THE SMELL OF COFFEE

I want to wake up some day to a coffee smell
twining like a creek through a pale yellow
early morning field of feeble light.
And see someone remarkably like you
with slept-in hair, housecoat half open
and practical flannel nightwear that makes
the glimpse of skin between two buttons
extra pleasant. Oh and I just noticed her
dainty bare feet, toes almost lost in carpet.
I see her eyes haven't been rubbed or washed,
the lids at half-mast, giving her a smoky
Lauren Bacall look. But mine keep returning
to her mouth, the way it's slightly open, the jaw
and lips not as yet fixed for the day, seeming
too trustful for someone of her experience.
When she leans on her arm along the door,
the housecoat opens further and the top lifts
slightly to reveal, in the weak light, down
on the stretched white flesh of her stomach.
Rubbing the back of one leg with the other foot,
she says *Was it my turn? I made some coffee.*
When we finally go to the kitchen, the smell
is achingly pungent. Tomorrow it will be me
in the door. If you will be the one who wakes.

SONG OF YOUR SKIN
for Sharon

Beneath my skin your skin
pebbles, puckers, ripples
and O the sensation
knowing you pulse within,

that my breath's enough
to summon your throat's blush,
that you hear the words I
sign with an eyelash on your thigh.

I can never see, never feel
enough of you – the moles, the mounds
that hold my bites,
the hollows, the fleshy rounds

that dimple
with the notion of a finger,
and that I cannot kiss without
a tremor.

My lips and tongue go mad
trying to take in
the lyric rise and fall,
the song of your skin.

THE WEDDING PHOTOGRAPH OVER OUR BED

In half-light, I see the photograph
in the mirror: white dress and hat
enclosing shadows on your face,

me nearly invisible in black suit,
a wing of white collar at my
throat, a retrospective flutter

in my heart. Each of our heads
leans to each as if teased with an urge
to touch, faces like candlelit

coins. By light's sorcery we change
sides. I transpose left. You move
right. Our clasped hands reverse their

holds. We've learned to make this switch
look easy, an occult
dance in which we trade more than places.

LEARNING THE LAND

We have failed each other. Let's not count the ways.
We're walking down a sandy prairie trail,
a new one we've taken on the way home
after the fireworks in town. It's long,
it's ordinary and it ambles like a stream.
A storm rumbles, one of us misreads the signs,
falters out of step and stumbles into
the weeds, alone, sore, exasperated.
It's been slow leaving the midway buzz,
trading the dazzle for moon and stars,
learning the lazy ways of hill on hill.
The detours around sloughs, and cautions
of thorns. So we floundered and forgave
and endured until the land was love.

OMAR BINNER, WIDOWER

With her gone
not just the bed
unbalanced –
my whole life,
like that playground
teeter-totter
she ran from
when we were kids
leaving me trapped
and scared
in the sky.

SPRING PARK

In spring the park greens with love. Hand in hand
and arm-wrapped amblers, nuzzlers in the grass,
benchers shouldering, the rusty squawk of swings
unwintering as boyfriends push girlfriends
into heavens of laughter. Just-planted violets
plucked and presented brighten new blouses.
Lawns fill with the smitten while overhead
in budding limbs nestlings totter and chirp.
The hobbler with his cane and wasted muscles
pecks wobbly along the paths, chin on chest,
inhaling his last April scentless through
a hole in his throat, his elbow cradled
by the woman who loves him in spite of,
on this the last of their green days together.

PHILOSOPHIC PATH

We strolled in the grove along the river.
She was young. I was old. Nothing
in that breezeless shadowed green
shone like her hair. She rued our human
faults, even the path we walked.
We spooked a porcupine who swung his tail
and rolled off. I donned a hardly worn
Rousseau. We held hands. We kissed.

She wanted a destination.
I discoursed on the forest path –
singular for two, a paradox of Zen.
We said things that have never been
repeated. That was...
I don't know when.

Now in this room allotted me,
the sunlight sectioned by venetians,
a few salvaged books stacked in
the wardrobe, over and over I tread
that day's path, thinking it may have
had a destination after all.

RETUЯN/FLIGHT

BIKES
for Miles

The garden sweet with dew,
a late cricket, a pair of waxwings,
a few cabbage butterflies
delighting the day as I
drag the bike from behind the shed.

My son is 32, this bike
23. We gave him a card:
your present is in the shed
and watched him beam as he swung
aboard, rode off on his first
big bike, a thin-tired blue ten-speed.

Now as I throw it away
beaten, twisted, rusted,
I imagine him dreaming of it
the way I still dream of
my first new bike, wheels of
distance and adventure,
tasteful red pinstripes
lining the cream fenders,
the caramel seat scraped
to the metal on the side
a truck squeezed me into
a brick wall in an alley.

I ride it all over town and
into the countryside.
I ride it forever.
My best bike riding away
the best of my days.

FET LOOKING DOWN

From his porch he saw the festival
in the darkness by the dam
where he and the guys had swum

They were celebrating the years
the city had survived
on the dry wide flatness

Old gangs were recombining
in the beer garden
laughing new legends into shape

He heard the hum of stories
from where bald heads gleamed
under the green lanterns

Dora shouted from the kitchen
For God's sake, Bert, go down
There's sure to be someone you know.

Beer in hand and shirt undone
he leaned against the door
blew smoke through the screen

No, he would not go down
to see what time had done
to people he'd hardly known

None of the guys was there
no one, now he was forty-two,
that he'd want to call him Fet

DEKE MAKES ROOM

He dies
the guy who sat across the aisle
all through high school
who swapped math and French
for your history and lit
who could always pot a long shot
when checked into a corner

He dies
whose whistling cool
made him first among the guys
the one you might have said you loved

And you recall his last time home
Scrawny, is that you behind the paunch?
Deke, is that you under that hairless dome?
reminiscing with beer and song
how you almost said it then

He dies years later in Toronto
and nothing leaves your life

So that now you have to force the fact
Imagine him humming over a snooker shot
driving in for a layup
smiling from the rim of a glass

Hammer and chisel it home
Gouge it deep into bone

He's dead

And at last an emptiness forms
the place that will be his

RETURN/FLIGHT

When you visit old calendars
the streets swim with the numbers
of your prehistoric sites

Familiar kids offer to find
the veiled maiden of the market
who once might have dated you

Merchants entice you with trinkets
divert you with alchemized
replicas of alien events

The voices you hoped to hear
in phrases from old scripts
have crawled inside your throat

and all the wonderful places
are flooded with death

Even the place of your drowning
your hometown's fat heart
is a foreign intersection

WHITE CRANE SPREADS WINGS:
THE TAI CHI CHUAN OF MEI-LAN LI

1. Maiden peers down path
Her friend San-feng says *Tai Chi
Chuan with Master Zhao is the way
to undo your squeezing stomach
and feel calm like lakes in summer.
Mei-lan, you are too full of trouble.
No good to look at soaps all day.
You must come to sifu Zhao.*
And Mei-lan whispers that she might.

2. Small child bends to story
Her mother told Mei-lan and now
she tells her only daughter Min
the tale Akeji, the merchant from Japan,
told their family long before the war.

*"Woman in Night River" explains
the weeping-woman sounds children
sometimes think they hear at night.*

*Travellers near a busy river crossing
hear nearby sounds of a woman crying...*

3. Woman leans on table
Mei-lan Li's shoulders tremble
as she swallows her sobs, not to disturb
Cheng-fu and Min. When she places
her head on her arms she winces
from the welt near her eye.

But she will go with San to Master Zhao.
It is not *wu*, not combat. He need not fear.
She wants to breathe the peace.

4. Master bows, students bow
First awaken the body. This is
Pick Up Mountain. Inhale – arms
arc up, and exhale – down. This
is Golden Fountain. Right palm
centred on tan tien. Keep
spine straight so shen flows up.
Next: Shooting Bow at Eagle –
inhale aiming, exhale after.
Now Shaking Head and Tail
Removes Fire From the Heart.
Next: Make Mad Eyes at Fists.

5. Woman weeps at crossing
Each night in haze of river breath
half-submerged among the rushes
she weeps for strangers to hold her child
so she may have small relief, some sleep.
Travellers approach, see no one, though
their reaching hands receive a bundle.
But when cradled, the child wails
half-choking, in dark silken layers
and she sweeps it back from sight,
and the travellers haste away.

6. Merchant makes mad eyes
Cheng-fu demands where she has been,
seizes her arm, draws her face to his,
You think Tai Chi can overpower me?
Mei-lan shakes her head looks down.
His nails bite into her. His laughter
full of liquor. *Go to the stupid classes,*
stupid little shaking bird. Next day,
each arm has an arc of finger bruises.

7. Woman holds single whip
Stop says Master Zhao and he
comes round to inspect stances
while they hold the Single Whip.
When he reaches Mei-lan he sees
the tremor in her hands, asks
if she is cold. Mei-lan shakes her head.
When he adjusts her pose,
his hands warm hers. She trembles
more. He whispers, *Your chi*
is choked in a thousand knots.

8. Sad woman holds child
Tales of the mysterious woman reach
famous palace warrior Ju-pai Chu.
One night in breast and leg plates,
with sabres, with spears, he rides
to the ford, hears the woman weeping.
"I have journeyed many leagues. Please
hold my child that I may sleep a while."
As soon as Ju has the child and hears
its muffled cries, he gallops away,
a voice behind shrieking like a demon.

9. Man grasps lotus
At Tran's, Cheng boasts that Mei-lan obeys
without a whimper like an old country wife.
The elders nod endorsement; the young study
their cards. Home, he lies about his losses,
accuses her of stealing from the house account.
When Mei-lan offers the budget book,
he flings it down. One hand clasps his buckle.
He stands scowling while Mei-lan shudders.
Then he laughs and hauls her against his body.

10. River breaks mountain
Master Zhao shows one by one
Mei-lan and the others how to push
and gather breath, how to make
all motions a simple single grace,
a river rising from wave to wave
that never breaks. *Nothing stays
the river, not even the mountain
it erases with soft embrace.*
They learn not to do Tai Chi,
but to let each move enact itself
as the breath of mind propels.

11. Soldier unwraps parcel
Mei-lan is surprised to hear herself
revising Akeji's story as she speaks.

*Ju-pai speeds to the palace to strut
his prize before the nation's nobles
assembled by rumours of his quest.
They swarm forward when he sets
the bundle on the banquet table.
He keeps his movements slow and
long to stretch the time he has their
eyes and so make greater the surprise.*

12. Maiden sidesteps snake
When she leaves Min's room Cheng is there,
tapping his palm with her favourite figurine.
He wants her to account for the missing
minutes that made her arrive from class
at nine forty-two instead of nine fifteen.
She explains that she and San had to repeat
some figures for Master Zhao. Cheng nods,
slowly replaces the figurine on the table.
Later, Mei-lan is amazed that under his sneer,
his hard-faced menace, she did not tremble.

13. White crane spreads wings
Left leg pivots left on ball
of foot. Lower left palm near
left hip as right foot follows
round and right arm rises
from waist to above right brow.

Mei-lan first feels the lightness
lift her during the White Crane,
moving from deep in waist up
to the roof of her skull, and yet
her legs and feet seem as one
through wooden floor with earth.
The lightness tickles through her scalp,
her hair. She cannot contain a smile.

14. Leaf drops in garden
When Min's eyelids close, Mei-lan stops.
Then Min's eyes open wider than before.

Silence now as Ju unwinds the silks,
one by one, layer on layer unswathed.
Between two folds, a few faded leaves
fall out, and with each unwinding more
and more flutter to the white stone floor,
cascading like an orchard in October.

15. White crane flies to nest
More careful now despite her joy
Mei-lan annoys San and declines
after class practice. Departing,
she thinks she sees a white moon blur
through the leaves – Cheng's Mercedes.

16. Embrace tiger, return to mountain
Mei-lan's feet, hips, hands move
in concert to music that sounds
like light through icicles in caves.
Her knees bend on their own, her
back stays straight and supple.
Her fingers spread and glide
as if around an unseen sphere.
Her mind conducts and yet
more and more soars free.
It rides her motions the way ravens
ply heaves of valley heat.

17. Leaves descend in rain
Someone laughed. Who laughed?
Ju turns, his forehead wet.
Silence. His hands tremble,
bump each other reaching.
More layers and more
leaves. In a fever now, Ju
feels wildly for the child. Grey,
beige, dull yellow, brittle leaves
drizzle through his fingers.

18. Young girl searches clouds
Mei-lan asks Min if she went for a ride with her father.
Min says no, she was bad, could not leave her room,
had turned her game on without permission.

Min alone. How long had Cheng lurked outside?
She must ask if Min can go with her.

Cheng says *Who cares?* Pleased she has a chaperone.

19. Waving hands in clouds
While her hands float and glide
Mei-lan imagines Ju-pai's plight,
victim of swagger and sword,
much-admired master warrior
suddenly by a woman's spell,
before his comrades, the fool.

The others turn. The music
of their movements broken
by an eruption of giggles.

20. Lifting hands to trees
More than Min, Mei-lan needs
the story now, enjoys making it
stronger. Min smiles to see
how much her mother smiles.

Ju-pai at last clutches the heart
of the bundle – a thicker twist
of leaves. Nothing but leaves,
no flesh, no life, no child to lift
in triumph. His ears burn with
smirking laughter. He roars
a wild elephant's gust of anger.
Leaves the colour of dusk, of old
men's hands, of dried blood,
cover the silver toes of his boots.

21. Young girl looks to sky
Min colours in the corner of the gym
making leaf pictures, looks up startled
when someone laughs out loud – her mother!

22. Golden cock stands on one leg
Without a wobble, she moves
on a strand of beauty,
a radiance.

This wonderful singing will
sing long and glad
its honey in her bones.

23. Riding horse to river
With taunts and laughter
swirling in his ears, Ju-pai,
his eyes red as the dragon's,
remounts his still-warm steed,
and screaming
speeds to the river.

24. Waving hands in kitchen
Reaching for a cup Mei-lan's
arm moves up/down into
White Crane Spreads Wings
and the smiling soars in her.
Her breakfast waiting, she
completes the form. Min
drops her toast to watch,
afterwards applauds.

Though forbidden, she cannot
resist. Waving Hands in Clouds
is moving through her
when Cheng enters.

Her smiling stokes his rage.
He slugs her to the floor.

25. Fair lady works shuttles
Though Master Zhao has many years,
his arms, knees, hips move smooth,
low and lithe as a child's. She will
move this easy way, like water, free.

The releasing flow of *chi* through hands
that weave twin lines with
ease. This is the way she needs
to be. She repeats it like a plea.

26. Listens for demons
Now Ju-pai believes a demon,
fox-woman lives in the river,
a weaver of illusions, clever,
with no fear of sword or spear.

Wary of serpent wiles, he
arrives to night fog, hears only
bamboo snicker, chuckle of water,
the rhythmic snigger of frogs.

27. Fair Lady hides treasure
Both palms flat on the table
Cheng hunches his shoulders,
and in his most venomous hiss
forbids any further classes.

Mei-lan pretends her old self,
glances silent down, doesn't
mention Zhao has announced
that a single lesson remains.

28. Repulse the monkey
Striding backwards one advances.
The illusion of submission
invoking the foe's assurance.

Practice please always this way
for good health and peaceful path.
Then you will have the gift of gifts.

Master Zhao and students, facing
each other for the last time, bow.

29. Searching bushes
Min wriggles and squirms,
with excitement.

Cursing, sword in hand,
Ju-pai crashes through the rushes
slashing left and right.

Fox-woman must be found,
must pay for his terrible shame.

30. Fair lady in storm
This is the most severe beating.
With Min locked screaming in her room,
he punches Mei-lan's face, rips her hair,
kicks her under the table.

Broken nose, broken ribs, bruises,
abrasions, finger burns on her throat.
A gash where the figurine shattered on her thigh.
Try your crazy dancing now, he snarls.

31. Bend bow and shoot tiger
Breath wheezes in her packed nose,
stitches and bandages bind,
body flames with pain,
but Mei-lan will do the form.
Not correctly but somehow.
Wincing, lurching, slowly
she drags through most of it
before the astonished San-feng
arrives, forces her back to bed.
Enough medicine for today.

32. Stepping into river
Min like a bird on the edge of the bed,
holding her mother's puffy hand,
protests but then agrees to hear
more of the Woman in Night River.

Ju-pai finds the very place
where he received the howling
bundle. Stabbing the darkness
he strides into a deep hole
and weighted by his armour
and the weapons he won't release,
Ju-pai bubbles to the bottom.

Min applauds. They both smile.

33. Wind opens heavy door
Twice Cheng stomps through the house.
Mei and Min gone. No note. No attorney.
On the kitchen floor, the broken figurine,
chunks of glass, Mei's pink scarf, blood.
On the counter the framed family photo.
Cheng hurls it into the chandelier.

34. White crane flying
Under the willow, a waxen leaf
spirals into the circle where
Min and Mei-lan, in white
blouses billowing over red
pyjama trousers and bare feet,
allow white crane wings
to lift them by feather
strokes inside their ribs.

They glide in echo of each
other in slow liquid measures
that blur like far-off voices
travelling a tranquil lake.

In violation of correct form
both are smiling.

35. Woman rests on shore
Was she a demon woman, mother?

No. Years ago she was pregnant
and died before the time, yet she
wanted so fiercely to bear her child
she would not leave with Death. So
each night she strained to deliver
her child to the living, until at last
its flesh wasted. Only crying remained.
Now she is released, now one hears
only night sounds on the river.

36. Sisters sway in garden
At last the child without a birth
dies and rides into peace. To praise
her deliverance, her sisters
dance together through the leaves.

BECOMING DEAD

1. The Syndrome
More of us acquire the ability
each season It's deafening
all the switches click off

Like those science fiction houses
with flowers in vases books
open food on plates

and no one home at all only
the breeze puffing curtains
a pale hint of presence

Hearing a voice you enter a room
and it's empty Voice after
voice Room after room

Someone pays the bills
trims the lawns and votes
as the polls foretell

Yet it's thought impolite
to point to where they were
even though the earth

is filling up with spaces

2. Case History
He is young. He is immortal. He
resides in the surface of his prefab face.
His clothes come with built-in lives.
He knows his bits and sticks to the scripts.

He flexes as required – squeezing, pleasing.
He seals his feelings in freezer bags.
He plods unfired. He concurs. He cripples
and acquires. If need be, he kills.

He views without vision. He shakes
in the calyx of a counterfeit flame.
He casts ashes at the sun. He looks good.
He does not notice how dark it is.

3. Acceptance
Gloss, floss, froth and fluff – O
the lightness of the brightness
will bubble you through
40,000,000 minutes of life.
Count 'em on your
tiny Texas Instrument.

All the fun that's the most fun
has now been filmed. You
can gorge while you watch
the dazzle queen of rock
boogie with the bishop
on the madcap late nite show.

Amazing how amusing the news is:
those people who combust,
the private lives of stars.
And always the clatter-patter
of the merry ping-pong balls
in the merry bingo halls.

Fun to dance to robotic tunes
as if you embraced more
than vacant space,
or to mate for the night in
a comic strip bed beneath
two empty balloons.

It's hardest for the living.
They must relinquish love
or the chance of love,
resign themselves, and enter
the cemetery dressed
as freshly closed holes.

OCCUPANTS

Each decade the nation relocates, blotching mailing lists
and address books, depressing the post office.
Houses empty and refill like tidal pools –
subsidized duplexes, custom-builts with decks and saunas.
Banks and realtors compounding a frenzy of profits
from lives in ebb and flood, the pulse of commerce.

Families appear in their sitcom windows, as if someone
were switching them on and off, a restless thumb on a very remote
control, new lives aligned in neighbourless neighbourhoods.
Troubled couples try new networks, workers move to places
where work must be better, the jaded seek cities to excite them.
The kids on a merry-go-round of playground counterparts,
parents grooming new yards, TV-numbed, dozing, nameless.

A husband dies, a wife escapes, a career withers, the cat is poisoned.
The moving van drops ramps, men in overalls struggle
under mattresses, pianos, refrigerators, precious boxes.
Hedges are planted, fences erected, swing sets come and go.

This searching for the proper ground, this uprooting
and transplanting to occupy what once were fields,
and woods where animals lived their lives entire.

This is how we flee and seek each other. How we mix
and sift the mysteries. These flights into our distances.

AUDREY
In memory of Audrey Johannessohn

Her massive hand crushed mine
as she boomed,
"Well, I've heard good things about you,"
then looked me up and down,
"but they musta been lies."

She never drove a rig but could have,
waited on tables in a border town,
salt and pepper shakers
trembling when she lumbered past,
listening to truckers' laments,
giving her tips to runaway girls.

"Had me a fifty-buck makeover once.
Looked like a goddamned movie star.
But who ever dates Lassie?"

Her cure for melancholy bards:
Stomp into a crowded lounge and roar,
"Hey, poet, you'd better thank me big time.
I saved your life a minute ago."
"How?" I ask warily.
"Ran over a shit-eating dog."

It was stupid when she died,
I couldn't help thinking,
Who's going to save me now?

NORTHLAND PRO

My father said the Northland Pro was the world's finest hockey stick.
This back when I was shorter than the boards on the outdoor rink
and he was skating for the Hornets. That's when he bought his only
Northland. Mother cursed it – a sliver of wood worth more than half
a ton of coal.

He showed me how to judge the lie, the grain, the splice, the shaft
for flex and strength, how to space and roll the tape and seal it,
sizzling, on the stove. To keep the moisture out, he varnished it,
then stood it, perfect and golden, by his equipment in the spare room.
At night when he was at work, I'd creep in and hold it, so incredibly
light and balanced, smell the mix of varnish, tape and wood and
feel the hat-tricks flying from its blade. Too beautiful to ice with
the cheaper hacking sticks, the gouging steel.

Each year, even after he'd hung up his skates and I wore them on
the high school team, he'd sip beer, add another coat of varnish and
talk to that Northland about what they could have done and might
yet do. But he got stuck on night shifts and rye and never did see
me play, even after he retired, the curved blade and fiberglass days.
When he died, the Northland passed to me. It sits in the closet of
my den, and once a winter, even now that I've hung up the skates,
I open a beer, take it out, dust the darkening wood, and tell it what
we might have done.

OLD MEN

Three old men on a front porch
gruff in rumpled sweaters,
coughing phlegmy coughs
while inside a boy struggles
with snarled suspenders.

The boy runs out three years later
and they both stand, arms crossed
on paunchy sills. One grumps,
You're twisted all bassackwards up.

Two old men on the front porch
dozing in undone vests,
snoring retorts,
a youngster inside sweating
to knot his first necktie.

When he strides out after four years
the old guy squints up
through hedgehog eyebrows,
Looks like two raccoons tug-o-warred your tie.

Old man on the front porch,
chins in tiers on his chest,
hands plaintive in his lap,
while inside a man combs
and combs recollected hair.

In five years when he plods out
the sun has nibbled the paint
from the empty chair.
Tired, he sits down.

WINTER

Snow-locked, she wakes alone
trembling on a finger of rock.

What was a stream recedes dead, pale
through shadows of hemlock and pine.

Untested lines dropped her here where she
must fight to deploy her gear and cling

to granite. This shield ice scoured from trees,
earth's glacial conquest.

And all her sun-ridden summers
have blazed to ashes in fading places.

She strives through heaps of trifles,
to inscribe a dark trail from

white. Burning itself, her flesh holds on
while the wind carves truth on her bones.

NOVEMBER WALTZ

Tonight a crystal-bright winter fog
flickers in moonlight above your graves,
and one by one you vapour forth
to flutter greyly in the air.

Mother, Father, the Grandfather I never
knew, and the one whose tweedy sweater
scratched my baby flesh.
Grandmother, Grandmother,
come up, come out and into my arms.

I'll be your boy, your son, your man,
whatever partner your hearts require.
We glide in tombstone-shadowed grass
as if falling into the old steps
pressed in the parlour carpet.

Look what I've become, you who feared
the dream-lost lad would never learn to work.
Look what I've become, you who thought
I was too frail or foolish, you who thought
I'd wear a uniform in danger or in a jail.

Have I got it, Father, have I got it
right at last? And, Mother,
may I have this last waltz?

Headlights strobe the leafless elms,
a breeze frets the fog,
and I discover myself alone,
arms full of vanished bones.

HAMMEL

HOW HAMMEL FLEW UPSTAIRS

Something from inside him
precedes him up the stairs
something vaporous
too small, too capricious
to be a guardian angel.

And certainly not a wish
or dream made palpable
by ardent tremors
of urgency luring him
skyward with a promise,

whatever that might be.
Creating a lightness
in the heart of his stomach
it slips out erratically
and wings a flight or two.

Ho-hum. More exuberance.
Another extrusion of ecstasy
and him with no excuse,
no ingested sparkle, no up-
lifting lore, revelation, tryst.

Just this cheek-bursting grin,
this eye-creasing galumphy
grin, declaring to any
who surprise him: harmless
but irretrievably raptured.

REMOTE CONTROL

Hammel has fallen asleep peering through the picture window of
an image by his friend The Poet. He wakes to the TV spouting news
of Diego Cardaenza who has strapped explosives to his lover's body.
Via cell phone while hovering over a laptop in his van, Diego threatens
to detonate her and the neighbourhood. His terrified lover, Suzette,
in view of him and the world, trembles on the balcony of her flat,
cellphone to her ear, her building and those nearby evacuated.
Helicopters whacking the air. Comely media commentators lathering
over the tactics of terrorism applied to a personal crisis. The special-
ops brass, cells pressed to their ears, consult with psychiatrists and
hostage specialists. Snipers and demolition experts consider how to
take him out in less than a pulse.

A commentator deadpans, "Science and technology make this moment
possible." Hammel is horrified and deeply empathetic. His attention
wanders to what would have happened if he had his ex wired thus.
Or vice versa. The temptations of remote control.

Something dark outside his window startles Diego. A cell phone on
a cable. Diego takes it inside, puts it to his free ear. He explains to the
police that he will not blow half their city to microspecks but, instead,
just neatly dispose of Suzette, if they will agree to charge him jointly
with her murder and that of the fetus she carries. "Now we know
what kinda nutto we got," says one of the cops.

A detective's voice tells Diego the cell phone could have been a
bomb that left him headless. Diego tells the policeman that would have
automatically blown up Suzette and most of downtown since
his van is trigger-packed with liquid nitrogen. The detective asks
him if he is hungry. He says he has lots of food and cigarettes.
Suzette wants an abortion? He'll give her an abortion. He'll
de-womb the whole damn city.

Hammel's phone rings. His friend The Poet wants some routine information. She knows nothing of Diego. "In the garden all day," she says, "tending sparse and prickly things that may well be weeds, watching bees turn into angels and back again, making notes." So he tells her all of it, the story of Suzette and Diego, the fetus and the police and the reporters and commentators on all the channels. He speculates on the many who have called in sick or returned from work and are now ordering pizzas so they will be watching when whatever is going to happen happens.

The Poet thanks him and says she is returning to the garden to watch the bees and the stars becoming leaves on her late April trees.

And there he is, alone with Diego and Suzette, growing uncomfortable watching himself watch them. So he goes to the window. It is the time of day when the shrubs lay down shadows longer than themselves. Something moves, almost hovers, near the lilacs. It may not be an angel but he hopes it is.

HAMMEL LOOKING

Hammel looking all his life to change
his life – burning bushes; grotto visions;
a poet resurrected singing strange
verses with quickening revelations.
An enchantress who will illuminate
the four tensions that wring him apart
simultaneously yet not dominate
his being. The stories, the plays, the art,
the music, the dance that could restore
the excitement they used to impart.
After Blake, Rilke, Yeats and Scotch galore
demolished his brain, not much surprises him.
The fireworks of poems in time grow dim.
Even those he kindled have become a bore.

HAMMEL PONDERS WINTER

September and the night wind
bites at the window
      Hammel
wonders about geraniums
does he have any
          does he have
a quilt or whatever warmed him
last winter
he tries to recall
the yellow eiderdown the gold
afghan the brace of grey blankets
where are the old comforters
now that all winters are one
under the shabby chenille

he thinks suicide
          not methods
dozens per room

the pros and cons
with winter growling up his pant leg

his mind scans last year's note
still under his shirts
          winces at
to whom it may concern

no changes   no additions

the arrangements who will do them
Myrna first cousin six Christmases
away
      the bankrupt state
him on the chopping block
transplanters queuing up for parts

well maybe not tonight
              winter might
not roar till after Halloween
and tomorrow there may be
geraniums to bring inside

SOUTH AMERICA

It's a Saturday night in January and Hammel is too tired to masturbate. Nor is he so inclined having just read a news story still open on the half-empty bed. Close-ups of a father and son rope-bound, bayoneted in roadside weeds, the blood dried maroon on their white short-sleeved shirts. According to the caption, the mother, tortured with fire, didn't break until the second murder, telling them something and saving, for a time, her other son. What does Hammel think? That death by misadventure with his .22 would be a treat compared to what this woman underwent? That there are things worse than being bald, fat and forty-two in a place where there are sixty TV channels and the powerful don't have to kill to get their way? Where all your knives are utensils or metaphors whose wounds permit you to enjoy chocolate sundaes and Fundador? That his knee-jerk compassion has suffered an over-extension? All of the above. In sequence. The woman is not in the picture, but he can feel the heat of her screaming, see her bend and clasp the small boy as if to crush him back into the safety of her womb. Her tears on his hair, his face. Then turning away to walk in her heart forever round and round the killing place. A ravaged widow in a ravaged land. And Hammel wants to fly there, and without speaking, shove aside the uniforms, take the boy in his arms and bring them back to the marvels of sixty channels and chocolate sundaes. To mere loneliness if they choose. He realizes his feelings are dangerous and stupid, an unfocused replica of love. This while sleep takes a part of him on what has become a Sunday morning.

HAMMEL GOES FORTH

Hammel rubs Grecian Formula into his beard and smiles his new smile hoping there is still hope. No one has loved him for years and sometimes he forgets to pretend he prefers it that way. Outside it is twenty-seven below and the wind skids over the dunes of snow and slams against the west wall. Hammel dreams of other men's women. The dark-eyed bare-shouldered temptress of the Pontiac commercial who the moment after the camera's click, flies into the photographer's arms. The cute waitresses flashing engagement rings above his burgers. The slim, suited briefcase toters sliding with sleek thighs into waiting Mercedes. How does it happen all that love? (Hammel you scruffy old gymbag, how can one so wasted sustain faith looking in your every morning mirror? How can you dream a possible marriage when the last time you really kissed anyone besides your ex was at that high school party when everyone was stoned and loved the entire earth?) And yet Hammel believes. Love can be. If only. And love when it arrives will not dwindle like his winter stock of brandy. As Hammel slogs to his Dodge his beard ices the new smile into place. Rigid behind the frosted windshield he listens to his motor moan and die. And still. He heads for the cluster of people at the bus stop. This could be the break. Maybe today, Hammel you old scruff-bucket, maybe today.

THE NOTES OF HAMMEL'S DOCTOR

Physical

Droops most days
like a snake sun-dazed
between two stones

Blind but highly responsive
to tactile & cortical stimuli

Ardently craves workouts
achieves few

Hydraulics semi-clogged
unpredictable
the golden bow
now a messy splurge

Psychological

Identity ambivalent
responds to various
names   Tommy Tentpeg
Mr. Upright   Crooked Dirk
Shazam   Captain Poker
& What Have We Here

Lengthy depressions
brief manic sessions

Elaborate attention-getting
behaviors, some inept
some ill-considered

Perks up when
acknowledged

Plagued by
inarticulate longings

Isolation-induced neuroses
fear of blemishes
fear of blades
sporadic stage fright
and mild attacks
of impostor syndrome
with dread of exposure

Tends to act impulsively
on slight provocation

Prone to falling
indiscriminately
thus often
inappropriately
in love

Treatment

More companionship
and emotional support
preferably by S.O.
but should take
whatever comes

Regular exercise
Psychotherapy
For aplomb
a placebo

THE IMPOSTOR SYNDROME

No one can tell he isn't there.
They come to the house or
the sub goes to theirs
or it goes shopping or out
for beers. And of course it
answers his phone and pays
his bills, forges cheques,
lies to friends, pretends
what they pretend, even takes
his pills and eats his meals.

In the attic Hammel grows thin
reading Rilke in bed, not
knowing the time, day, month,
drinking brandy, remembering.
The sub's daily reports
become monthly memos.
He never knows where it is.

He never knows when it will
tote the shotgun up the stairs
and simplify their lives.

NOT TODAY

Another day he didn't die
and Hammel leaks gratitude
in the general direction of
a divine beneficence.

Not being dead is the best way
to enjoy life's antidotes –
TV, books and movies,
traffic-free late-night drives.

The storm outside would freeze
his blood before he sneezed,
but natural gas, insulation,
wood and wool save his life.

So now, alone in the house,
he sings his awful version
of "Wonderful, Wonderful"
and waltzes with his winter coat.

He sings himself a wondrous life
of warm, concocted memories
a sweet and tender paradise
of Hammel-centred love

that might have been love
had he not been Hammel –
a crazy, crazy moon-crazed bat
he sings and drops in a chair.

*Failure's the only thing you've
not failed at.* Whereupon
he laughs his laugh and declares
he's earned another Scotch.

HIS DODGE

The car takes Hammel beyond his intentions.
This morning beside a field of flax in bloom
turning sullen blue in the pre-sun sky
was yesterday's trip to the pharmacy.
Now he is out of gas, out of road.
He has turned the wrong way so many times
chasing country music into darkness
he judges he's a few miles south of Sorrow
near Hopeless. The light tells him he's east of home.
His heart tells him home is just a song
in the night. His Dodge slants into the ditch,
locked in reverse, its mirror full of regrets.
His rifle leans against the far door.
Soon a voice will bring directions.

HAMMEL ATTEMPTS SLEEP

He climbs into the bed where he expects to die,
Old Hammel who never made a stick's worth of
trouble and for whom no one is likely to cry
since he failed with great frequency at love.

Old Hammel, who never made a stick's worth of
trouble except his own which he made double
since he failed with great frequency at love,
tried all his life and seldom rose above rubble.

Trouble, except his own which he made double,
other men managed far more deftly while he
tried all his life and seldom rose above rubble
Contacts! said a sage *will assure supremacy.*

Other men managed far more deftly, while he,
working as hard as he could, was submediocre.
Contacts! said a sage *will assure supremacy.*
When once he found a princess his kiss never woke her.

Working as hard as he could, was submediocre
in all he pursued – that's what life brought him.
When once he found a princess his kiss never woke her.
The first woman who showed an interest got him.

In all he pursued – that's what life brought him –
one relationship that never found a focus.
The first woman who showed an interest got him
and her love shrivelled faster than a crocus.

One relationship that never found a focus.
Hammel, who knew it wasn't his doing only
and her love shrivelled faster than a crocus,
now finds himself a year beyond lonely.

Hammel, who knew it wasn't fate bringing only
trouble and for whom no one is likely to cry,
now finds himself a year beyond lonely.
He climbs into the bed where he expects to die.

MYSTERIES OF EVERYDAY LIFE

TECHNIQUE

The trick is not
in leaping far enough
from the frozen path

nor falling down
like a timbered tree

nor fanning your arms and legs
through the thick snow

no
the real trick
is getting up
and getting out
leaving not a trace
to tell
which angel fell

REHEARSALS

This blindness could be foreseen.
He was mad for the feel of things –
the sleek sheen of porcelain,
the brittle crystal of crusted snow,
inner thighs, their silken skin.
Eyes closed always.

In the cellar he'd file his fingers,
skin dusting to the earthen floor.
Slide hands alive in the gloom
along the shelves of preserves,
the broom, the shovel, cool
jagged fragments of coal.

Each room a song. Bath-soft fingers
along the bristles of a brush,
the lushness of towels, the shiver
of chrome fixtures. Eyes closed
for focus, naming each sensation,
rehearsing absence.

Today hearing Peterson play
he sees hands on the keyboard,
feels the moonlight of the keys,
the rough edges of furious riffs.
This blindness a room of blooming hands,
touching, retouching, subtle as leaves.

VACANT AFTERNOONS

1. Present
Snugged to the earth, his open eye
sees a small stone, pink with black flecks,
the base curved like a keel casting
a pointed shadow. It rests on granules
of reddish soil, though a few in the light
are crystalline. He cannot escape it,
locate the inner place he has vacated.

No ant on the back of his neck
as he had thought, but sweat starting
to trickle from his hair. Against his ribs,
his arms are numb, one hand tingles.
He is unsure about his legs. Earlier,
sounds turned hazy, stopped.

When he stands and wipes the earth
from his forehead and cheek, light will
slam his other eye, blackbird and wind
sounds and the stream's sloshing
will burst into his ears, and sorely
his legs and arms will rouse back to routine.

Knowing that, he remains longer,
attempting return,
locating sensations and one
by one unhooking them, waiting
for the purity of perfect disconnection.

2. Past

Memory finds a Sunday when
the late afternoon sun continually
dissolves in cloud and reappears
east of one o'clock. He is doing
nothing. On his belly watching
red ants scurry. On his back to see
a hawk disappear in the sun. At
the creek to scoop and drop handfuls
of minnows. Not aware his new
clothes are hand-me-downs. Not
aware he is alone. Not thinking
anything. This is the afternoon
the fox steps from the tall grass,
gazes at him, then prances off.
And the blue-green dragonflies
helicopter in the bulrushes while
the Vs from two slow muskrats
touch and lazily overlap. All the
trivial sensations sliding down
the sides of memory into this day.
A wheat grass stem sucked white
tasting of wind and heat and dust.
None of it going anywhere. He isn't
going anywhere. The day repeating
itself and the boy becoming a boy
into dazzling blue infinity.

3. Future
His memory purged and
replenished precisely as he wished,
his drift to romantic folly
reduced to a docile urge.

Images and words flow from his eyes
onto bygone screens,
the pages of forgotten books;
lyrics, their coy melodies, spill
from his ears into antique radios –
pillage from the grey museum
that induced replicas of love.
His rue an echo in marble.

He holds his arms to the sky
the way one hoists a child in joy
and feels the lift and peel
of lovers leaving, the cool
thrill of air on his chest,
lips numb, fingers tingling.
The flit of dragonflies in reeds
where blackbirds sing.

A distant heavy door slams
and reverberates in vacancy.
Silence, then, immaculate.

FALSE SPRING

Early March and already
something like spring
is teasing the garden.

Snow melts to puddles
in holes where the potatoes
were unearthed and the wind

rattling the raspberry
bushes is warm enough
to raise sap.

The maple, where for years
I planned to build my sons
a tree house, is mature and

dreams downward releasing
delicate fibres
to prime the flow.

I've imagined too many false
springs into myths of
summer. I gaze at

the garden this morning
the way my sons
sometimes look

at me, trying to conjure
approaching seasons.

BERRIES

My blueberries
in your white bowl
wear a silver mist thin
as sparrow's breath.

Where the breeze licks
they turn late-evening
blue. Between our teeth
they burst sweet and cool.

We eat them on the patio
while you speak of futility –
the litany of what could
have been yours if only.

After fifty prairie winters
you are beautiful,
which reveals your time
is yielding as it should,

and this crush of berries
in our mouths is
celebration enough
as evening slides west.

GRAPE

It's not large, this grape,
the size of a marble.
It rolls along my teeth,
submitting its flesh
in supple resistance.

The vendor said this batch
of red grapes came
from Spain. I imagine
Valencia, lush fields
fading into blue hills.

There, grapes may be red.
At the fruit stall, where
they bulge
in nets like pendulous
ganglia,

they're a dusty crimson
with splotches of smoky
grey and dull green
as if the limpid outer
skins encased an olive.

Flipped by my tongue
the grape flicks off the roof
of my mouth with
a hollow smack
like a ball in a game.

Under tongue, in its
moist nest, it dreams
summer, sunlight,
the anonymity
of uncountable numbers.

From the fridge, it was
cool but now
it has the warmth
of my body. When I
choose to bite down

the soft rupture will
flood my taste buds
and I will feel my own
heat the way a tiger
eating me would taste it.

BODY SONG TO HYPNOS

His body knows what it
wants, roams frazzled through rooms,
rejects TV, snacks, books,
the pill-launched phony doze
with vain shallow wipeout
and day-long after-grog.

Body wants what he knows
he hasn't had for years –
nights of dream-laced sleep,
the blizzard of longing to stop
exposing faces, and subside
to a soothing veil of flakes.

He studies the ways cats
laze through seven-hour days
and snooze in languid ease.
Body yawns in envy at subway
riders snuggled in sweaters,
careless mouths agog.

Hypnos, in your island cave,
god of sleep, sun-taker,
son-maker, listen
as he mumbles hymns.
Sleep fixer, sweet healer,
grant him a week's soft snows.

MYSTERIES OF EVERYDAY LIFE

1.

Inside the library's *On Becoming
a Novelist* by John Gardner I find
a crinkled black and white photo –
a thin-legged blonde in panties
and chemise smiling delectably
while holding an open umbrella
behind an unstrapped shoulder.

Did she make it as a novelist, or
did her lover, the one who so
casually left her in the section
about the personal sacrifices
of writers? Did Susan Swan or
Robert Kroetsch have this book
before me? The librarian says
they don't keep such records.

2.

Memos from "King" on the Co-op
bulletin board. Tacked amidst
auction notices, misspelled ads
for hardly used bicycles, like-new
waterbeds: *I'm still waiting* printed
above his name in quotations. A wit
once scrawled *What for asshole?*
underneath one of these.

My last encounter with any King
was a friend's long-tongued dog.
He would prance after whoever
spoke to him until he was chased
home. I have a vision of this
Irish setter in sunglasses, long
curved tail jutting through
his trench coat flap, striding in

on hind legs, and posting the note.
Maybe he wants to let survivors
of the old neighbourhood know
he's ready to romp once more.

3.
On my doctor's door, perhaps eight
inches from the floor a mouth
floats on the glossy varnish,
a perfect scarlet kiss, the kind
that used to make me ache
when left in the bathroom by
someone's girlfriend, pressed soft
on Kleenex or glossy on the mirror.

Was my doctor up to some down
and dirty on-the-floor grappling
with a very nearsighted blonde
in panties, chemise and umbrella?
Or was it the door-maker's woman,
after months of neglect, leaving
a souvenir kiss with his real love
positioned over sawhorses?

4.
The way parts of our lives break
off and drift into other lives.
Our most painful intimate
moments theirs to lift to their
lips like a kiss on Kleenex.

MOTIVES FOR BEAUTY

1.
The tiger is beautiful
in order to kill –

a liquefaction
of sun in the jungle

sinuous with shadows,
sensuous in vines.

In the half-light of leaves
he is what you do not

see before being slammed
down, the pain that ends

pain. Your flesh, your blood,
the price of beauty.

Your brain, silvery gel
inside its cracked shell,

the artist, the priest.
Without your sacrifice

beauty would starve
eating shadows on a limb.

2.
The violet is beautiful
so insects will pander

to its lust. Shape
colour, texture, combine

in the beauty we admire,
traits of curve and line.

And we fabricate so we
can muster praise,

pleasure, ease, honour,
plunder, power.

First delight is pure,
an interval of joy

before a claim is made,
before a flash of light

lunges from midnight
onto the hunter.

THE WORK OF SNOW

Forgetting is folded into snow,
the letting go of chronicles.

In the heaping whiteness,
flake by flake, faces grow pale,

the way these plains forget
trees, or the old woman

her first lover. The sites of crimes,
trampled black, are cleaned.

Blood flows onto snow, fades under
glaze and wanes in May to water.

There is always a last bout of sleet
then sun and once again

she begins to garden.

CASEY QUINN'S BEATITUDES

Certain as pre-dawn air is sweet
and sedate just waiting for a breeze
at the lower lake in May, it's there.
Or when the months are three
and four-syllabled so they can bear
hushed carols of snow-pure birth.
And when dusk smoulders down
it's there. Whether in dank
or thirsty air, in pinewood glens
or the scrawl of wind on shoals.
Even on the raven's open wing
gleaming vermilion, plum
and jade in the squint of sun.
Fresh as the smack of spring
on the cheek of stale March days,
it's there, to be sure. And not in your
fine briefcase, lad.

                    And so partake.
Crush darkness and ignite a screen
of peacock, cardinal and canary
fireworks that expire like sparks
in your lap, trajectories perfect
as well-packed buttocks. Why talk of
your "secured retirement savings"
with this dazzle in your middle?

Soak yourself in succulent oils
till your skin opens and craves
kisses, the exquisite carpet-crush
under supple foot, the crisp nip
of linen sheets, the singe
of skin, lips that render all
your flesh tender as nipples.

Your breath,
the sibilant rush of it in moist
pink passages, your body filling
with it like a lover receiving
love, the familiar miracle
of its lust for oxygen, the zing
of its leap from pulse to revel in cells.
Great god what glorious beasts
we be. What peaks we sing from
and sure enough yes descend aching,
spent, ready to savour repose.

Music,
art, books and food that burst
on us, in us like lunatic seeds,
their increase teasing modesty
to recreate their first embrace.
The luscious dishes we devise,
the lure of them, fragrances
that quicken or soothe. Ah, these
sweet comrades of solitude.

Goggle now at this canvas while
the first allegro from *Le quattro
stagione* sparkles: A Glendalough
stream all mossy stones and silver
flow before dusky trees. That vague
sunglow smudge on tilting clouds –
such natural accord, great god.
That artist, the famed Anonymous,
and Vivaldi lilt in concert,
both dead long ago and stowed
like brutes in peasant graves.

And where was time with its lists
and missions all that while
we gazed and listened there agog?
Out of mind. Mind, too, its play
and passions, the way just then
I mentioned the pauper burials.
How I wonder did those primates
ever come to think up thinking?

Memory and sorrow, too, the flit
of thoughts, their melding
into restless swarms – dream,
reverie, vision, fancy – like small
rainforest birds every tone and tinge
darting on amethyst, indigo,
ruby lines that never tangle.
Reason weaving designs, riddling,
clutching its crown, resolving
snags, inspecting calendars
so the griping bills get eased.

Or into the droop of hammock
letting the old head's bric-a-brac
surface randomly, or sensations
shrill their razzmatazz.
But cleansed of fuss and hum –
a lone leaf on the brow of summer
in a pond. Isn't it so, the mind,
bliss master, captain of cages?
It's true, I love my brain more
than chocolate or Kerry's brew.

In winter when the sun shouts
flat and hot through that big front
window, I strip me down naked
to thrill the widow across the way
and stretch out and bask in it
with my dog Bock. And so we wag
away many a warm afternoon
reading, sleeping, scratching.

Ah, legs, of course. How they look
and work, what a blessing
they are, legs. A symphony
is walking, such harmonies
of muscles, tendons, ligaments,
the architecture of foot –
toes, arch, heel, the physics
of knees and hips moving me
on these levers to my lover's
lips or off to fetch with Bock.
I like to be at pools or beaches
where I can gaze at legs unclad.
It's near to watching a child
asleep all nuzzled in a basket,
or the fish-scale sky at dusk
off Dunmanus Bay in Cork.

Bram and Ria come by, or I'm
to them, or we're to Kerry's
for a pint and sometimes the talk
zings along so tangy, it's sad
I am to leave and wring the snake.
It's art the way we waltz a point,
together but opposite, sure to rebut
whatever's voiced just to tease
ourselves from the slug of custom.
And being out or in with them
or the others is great god a wonder.
And being alone before or after,
with Bock gone to panic cats,
is as well a wonder.

            Partake, then.
Here's two foamy ale for us to share.
Or go amass money, polish your spoils,
pump your pickle and despair.
There's too much common miracle
to waste it glazed and puggled.
Fill each instant over-brim. Let
spill the perils. Look, I lick them yet.

THE WINTER MOTHS

1.

Novembers
cling unseen on earthen walls
and the undersides of clouds
cluster in numbers
so large and dense
cumulus skies
turn dingy as stones.

Thus are they called
"Four-winged Melancholy."

Thus when King Elam
of Persepolis
crushed November envoys,
(sent to seek agreement on
breeding by his streams)
hordes of them cast murk
and spread such woe
his soldiers became forlorn
and were slain.

2.

White Decembers,
small and quick,
are taken for flakes
of snow, specks
of frost.

Dime-sized
Decembers glaze
playground swings
and slides, poles
and wire fences.

They are so swift
and sly, fleeing
by rows into the sky,
sun-squinting
children think
spring.

Through days of
long nights
their shaggy feelers
tickle sleepers into
dreams of love.

Older couples,
hemmed with snow,
when stroked
with their plumes,
wake aroused
and make
long
August love.

3.

Januarys are dark and large with strong sucking tongues.
As revealed in ancient Thracian texts, Januarys,
working in concert, lifted Alexander and his horse
Bucephalus over Taurus peaks from peril in Cilicia.

It was swarms of Januarys pierced the veins of
the commanders of the Hindu Kush and their elephants
and spat their blood to freeze on cold Khyber slopes
giving that region spiked scarlet sunsets.

4.
None is more elusive than moon-winged
February, Luna's paler kin. None more
Beautiful. The translucent membranes
Of her ivory wings have sea-green veins.
Her nocturnal flights are rare surprises
Of such bliss beholders never speak again.
Nor do they care, for they are graced to fashion
Instruments from shell and sinew, wood
And wire, that place in air, for a lyric's length,
Half a ghost whose eerie spell they half recall.
Their music is of such delicate strength
There are few on earth it won't enthrall.
All the myths of air – echoes, sylphs and fairies –
Begin with recollected Februarys.

BEGINNINGS
Jan.1, 2001

After an hour of Bach, he
listens to a radio program about
the prevalence of human kindness,
the importance of perspective,
how after a terrorist blows up
230 people, over 13,000
dig out survivors, donate
blood and money, help rebuild.
The numbers start to add up,
to nibble his pessimism.

Beginnings are always
beginning. Animals becoming
human and more and more humans
looking more like God.

The networks haven't noticed,
nor the shoppers thrashing for
comfort. But mountain villages
and midwest towns are swelling
with unhaloed saints.

Tree branches droop with
angels asleep on each others'
shoulders like exhausted lovers.
Their grace falls everywhere.
like pollen from a divine distance,
germs of possible miracles.

SHE DIRECTS HER SELF-PORTRAIT

Wide lens the water and shoot low angle pans
towards those hills out west. Catch them
at dusk. Try to get the sun when it spokes through
the spruce. The shoreline is perfect
but rake those tire ruts. That road sign
is out, the litter, the beer cans.

These poplars, how they lean to the water,
like dragons in thirst, like green waterfalls –
can you shoot them in profile, and the dapple
of them on that shimmering surface?
Lots of that. The way those columns of light
tremble on the trembling water – shoot
that. Mid-morning for the sharpest
contrast.
        Over there, the waves in that oblique
stretch of light on the lake, see how they make
horizontal pleats that waver like ribbons?
Get those. Use the boat but keep it right out
of the shots.

            The incarnations of water.
Snouts of it that nudge and lick
the shore. The wake of its wet retreat
on the beach. Moonlit mud, slick in the pale
gleam. Shells in wet sand. The slosh among
rocks. The sheen on rushes and ferns. Rain, too.
We need rain, thick, straight down,
sleek in leaves with a grey light

in the distance. Let them feel wind. Its rush
in the valley. Grasses that thrash, manic
bushes, a chaos of branches. Wind
scrubbing the air. Easing in time to a whim
that plays in the reeds.

Then lights out. Night. Lake-honed
echoes. Tremors of owls. Older trees
moaning. The riffling of leaves. The suspicion of
paws. Rustlings. The moon liquefying
these. Later the silver of loons and

                              peace.

Nothing human. Not even a bench or a fence.
Only this lake, only this place.
                        Shoot a day,
a night, then strike, load up and fade
out.

NOTE TO THE WOMAN WHO DANCED IN THE PARK TODAY

You never saw me. Lost as you were
in what must have been the rapture

that fixed the sun in your smile,
and took you off the asphalt walks.

You waltzed through the park's
long grass, feet flashing and diving

like fish in and out of the shadow
waves beneath the trees, your blue dress,

your flaxen hair trailing in the breeze.
It seemed you hardly stopped to don

your shoes, pointing dainty toes in each
and gliding up the street, a dream

that every public park should have.
I don't know what life you stepped into –

a dancer when the dance is done –
but there must be music there and love

and if not, all the more your miracle,
all the more do I give thanks for you.

(I was the lean, bald one who seemed
to be reading a book by the gate.)

CHILD ЯUNNING

THE WILD YIRD-SWINE

They come at night, the wild yird-swine, and fret the graveyards
hereabout. Squat, dark brown splotched with black, slobbery
snouts and coarse hair all over, the sort as might sprout
in a dead man's ear. May have been domestic once some
centuries back, no one knows. They pack the weight
of a farmer well fed, and bite clean through a walking stick.
The stench of them's the sort makes fragrance of a corpse.
Young ladies, caught late on errands, chancing just the scent
of one, have crumpled like violets in the hot summer sun.
Even those that dig graves cannot abide the wild yird-swine.

Their hooves are extra sharp and smithy-hard, right for digging
the flinty soil that keeps the local pits a sorry shallow depth.
Their fondness is new graves, so loved ones pack rocks thick
and set a watch as long as half a year or more. They root up
coffins and bash their way inside the wood soft with rot,
and guzzle what remains of our relatives and friends.
Bones and all, the keepsakes, too, placed in love, a necklace
or a watch, unchewed bits of which will decorate their scat.
Not the sort of beast as you would set to play with children
or call to heel. Safe to say no one laments a dead yird-swine.

Though they must breed as hot as boars in the woods,
you never see a pair. Some say it's because they work in fours,
three sniffing sentinels while one does the grunty work,
their warning shriek beyond what human ears can snag.
Yet single sightings aren't so rare, even on a winter's eve,
the frozen earth an armor plate. Never so many though
as a few springs back when rain on rain made such floods
the streets were streams, and the old cemetery, half up
Sundown Hill, pitched forth at least a dozen caskets,
like rotten teeth in runny gums, for the wild yird-swine.

They scab it up and throw it in our faces – death. Ugliness
from ugly deeds arises. Treats for pigs – what sort of fate
is that for one whose pretty eyes turned eyes, or the man
whose art won every district prize? Oh, it's a desecration
and we ought to slaughter them. We do when we can, bury
them shallow for their own to find. But isn't death itself
the rankest sin and desecration? In the end, we don't want
to succumb to earth, to let it have its way with us, its crawlers
and vermin. If death's a levy in some plan divine, then the boon
had best be more than the gashers of the wild yird-swine.

MILDLY MANIC:
A POET MEETS JOHN NASH IN
MCLEAN HOSPITAL, BOSTON, 1959

1.
No confession, a depiction of a common condition,
to say I was not myself when I met Nash.
Is anyone ever fully himself and if so when?
Nor was he himself, tormented half the time,
muttering into his shoulder. We've misplaced ourselves
in this loony bin for the nation's Brahmin
where one is inspected, injected, restrained, debrained,
edified, medified, mental blocked and electroshocked.
I said that.
                He said you think rhyme makes sense.
It's merely a false algorithm. I don't recall my response.
I think I slandered numbers. A long silence
after that. It was in one of the corridors
that our symptoms first mingled like vapours.

P.S. When recovering, from time to time,
unpredictably, I relapse into rhyme.

2.
I suspect our duck-billed psychiatrists
conspired a non-paranoidal plot to couple us so
we'd each cancel the other's derangement,
balance at last the two irrational equations.

Our uncommon encounter was in the common room,
me in flagrant jabber, Nash nodding and peering
at my slippers, not listening, not talking at first.
Becalmed with Thorazine, or so I thought.

He reeked of smoke that evoked my uncle's parlour,
men propped with pipes and cigars explaining
what was wrong with my father.

I had to tell him I had lied about the juicing,
as we call the electroshock treatments.
Since Stanton took over a few years back
all that voodoo had been vanquished.
I gave him my spiel about faking
one's way through psychotherapy
and the rights of those forcibly committed,
Oh, that perked him up considerably.

3.
                    The door, the baseboards,
the window frames are painted spring-tree green
to soothe agitated brains. The paint has splintered
and the shreds collect in the unswept corners
like leaves waiting to become metaphors.

I think that it should be recorded for history
though it didn't seem historic. History seldom does.
Quaint the way Eisenhower thinks the future
will read his golf scores. Such a hole-in-one.
When I get snide like that I know I'm on the mend.
Maybe Nash perked me after all. I remember now:
I suggested that he not fire integers at a rhymester
with *trash, hash, crash, bash* and *smash* in the wings.

Flaunting his math biceps, he tried to demonstrate
the "simultaneity of the universe," muttered about
"an infinite regress," scribbled hieroglyphics,
more symbols than numbers, parentheses galore.
When done, he claimed he'd elaborated (and improved)
someone's proof that time does not exist. I couldn't resist
asking why the watch on his wrist. His answer was
something about the linear bias of the brain.

Should we care if time is a figment or myth? We are born.
We die. Things happen in between. If there is no sequence
of moments to divide events, as Nash asserts, what does?
If time's a mirage, we still damn ourselves to its confines.
If there is no early or late, how did I miss supper last night?
Without before and after how to measure my recovery?

I think he's haunted by echoes of zeros.

4.

He fell into another silence when I observed that while
I understood none of his scratching, his words indicated
that he was confusing the non-transitive verb to be
with the mathematical symbol for equals and that
to say Nash is tedious, is not to say Nash is tedium.
In other words, he finally said, you reject this proof
on the same basis as contemporary metaphysicians
reject the ontological proof of God's existence,
because it makes being a verb rather than a pure
copula attributing a quality and not a category.
I allowed as God could be a verb, a noun, a dishrag
for all I knew, that ontology is as ontology does,
and metaphysics begets inanity/insanity,
not to mention indolence, intolerance, and indigestion.

I suspect he's a genius in his own tree but germane
retorts are not his forté. He called me a hack
and dove into a calculating silence.

5.
Dancing over time we smash into God.
It starts when he says that God occupies
reality only in the mind of man. Ah ha,
I say, and does the mind not partake of the real
and therefore by virtue of the principle of containment
is God not real? He chuckles. *Thank you. You have*
just endorsed the so-called illusory creatures
whose presumed non-existence landed me here.

At last a retort worthy of his pretensions.
He may be loony but his mind ain't porridge.
We get to discussing how one tells the real
from the unreal. Nash's gestures become livelier.
I have always thought it foolish to try proving
God's existence by using the brain, so like
the chair trying to deduce the carpenter.
The brain itself is the best evidence –
its complexity, its alacrity, its capacity.
I love my brain even when she stomps my heart.

6.
Nash is puzzled by poetry except as a game.
I quote Lycidas, Lord Weary, extemporize.
Verse is corpuscular in me. One thinks of *curse*
or *adverse*, some flimsy spider wit on which
to rig the water-skin illusion of control.
The grand affliction of writers,
their blank pages being divine slates
for meticulous mistakes,
poets the worst, their mirage that they
have ordered every syllable for the best.

They age into righteous certitude
like Nash's hierarchy of mathematicians.
Three or more comprise a school or,
when at Yale or Harvard, a pantheon,
their babbling proclaimed on minion wings,
their technologies infallible.

The omniscient point of view seeps backward
from our pens into our veins
deluding us into thinking we understand
the nuances of brains like Nash's,
and though to the manor born, I detest this gall.
The all-knowing garble. The anemic omnipotence.

I renounce control. The tidy generic stanza.
The poet who deliberately plans a
long rhyming extravaganza
makes me want to vomit. (He bans a
temptation to use *bonanza.*)

Oh, I'm a bowl of healing confections
rife with bilious infections.

7.
When I'm mildly manic, as this week, I squeeze
my hands between my knees and exercise
restraint sufficient to convince the shrinksters
I'm in recovery mode.
                              I write letters, verse, notes
to strangers, stairways, trees and post them
in the latrine.

Manic, I can work magic. Translate a book a day,
over night jot an entire play.
                              Manics generate
the most progress in the least time with the highest
collateral grief. We are the agitated hearts of the world
beating triple time.
                              O rip us up. O rip us out.

Love wilts while we chicken-trot obsessions.

We charm or agitate the sane, amaze bystanders.

Last night a memo to Nash:
You are not crazy, John. Your brain has children
illegitimately and you legitimize them
with attention. Ignore them and Herr
Brain Doctors will do the same for you.
                              I don't
expect he can. He will be here when I return.

In sessions I am semi-calm, but not
serene, not the pill-graded blotto mind.

I could untether and explode all over McLean,
but I want a discharge.
                              Time to walk in time again
with a sweet tremor where once a tempest
vexed the workings in the old clock tower.

CHILD RUNNING

12 years now
the child has been running
legs/arms/hair aflame

The tears in her footprints
have dried The helicopters
have been sold for scrap
The captain who made the strike
hawks life insurance in Maine

Perhaps you've had enough of this
This is left-wing propaganda
It never really happened

yet we who saw her running
see her sometimes still
all of her aflame
like an angel
down the dusty road
with the wings of her screaming
swept back to us

LIAN LIAN

1.

Though the sun in Sichuan province
has been thin with fire smoke all day
Lian Lian removes her garments
leaves them in the reeds and bathes
in the Wu Jiang's warm waters.
It is her place, her time for cleansing
with palm oil soap wrapped in cotton.
She stays out of the current's grip,
keeps her legs bent to submerge
her breasts, her shoulders, her neck,
scans the land for the hats of men.

It is now a ritual, the way she rubs
her skin red especially between
her legs, then swims back and forth
stopping often to listen for
herdsmen and the thudding water
buffalo of the sugar beet farmers.

Lian Lian slithers from the water
up the slope of long marsh grass
surrounded by bushes and beside
her garments soon falls asleep.
Later, she could not recall if she
dreamed again of the brick plant men
their calloused hands, the pain.

2.
She told the gawking doctors she awoke
in a haze, wanting but unable to turn
on her side. She was held firmly from
knees to stomach by the python's fat coils
thicker than her thighs, the beautiful
gold-black-silver design winding away,
like a great banyan root down the bank.
Water droplets gleaming on its scales.

The amber-eyed snout shoots from beneath her
ribs and across her chest snaring one arm.
She feels her legs and hips being crushed.
She can manage only quick, shallow breaths.
She opens her mouth wide to risk a scream
but when the glistening head slides over her
shoulder, the wet black tongue flicking against
her cheek, without thinking, she bends forward
and bites down deep and hard just behind an eye.

She tears through the scales, rips away
a piece of flesh, moist and cold and tasting
like green bark. She spits it out. Then her head
spins and a long darkness falls upon her.

3.
Her bruised flesh as vivid as the creature's
under more hands, more instruments.
No faces, just voices – father, brothers,
nurses. A mist of whispers:

Swimming alone
    What man will

                                  Wrong

Not a snake
    People are saying

                                  Wrong

Demon lover
    Perhaps die

                                  Wrong

No man will ever
    Deserves

                                  Wrong

Day four she starts to moult. They pull silken
husks of skin, one a buttock perfectly
curved. Her hand hanging gossamer from
the nurse's hand. During the third, the last
moult Lian Lian, her fever gone, eyes open,
does not speak but sings, in throaty wobble,
love songs to the serpent.

                    The science men
are confounded and begin again to test.
Why has the fearful girl become so sunny?
Instruments once more, tubes and samples.
Once more the latex hands. Though now Lian
Lian smiles, knowing they will never know.

DANICA AT THE GOYA EXHIBITION
for Elly Danica

1.

Doctor Arrieta worked wonders and Goya lived
several more years. Your first doctor is your father
when you are four playing his special secret game
between your legs. There on the floor you want to die.
At the end of the street the moon is so full and huge
walking into it would be how you could escape
from his demands, his probing hands. Dream
of the moon, dream of being free and clean
on the dark side where he will never see, safe
in a cool moondust place. Beyond his camera's greed
for your body. What does he do with the pictures of you,
"the examinations" legs spread, or bending over his bench?

The well-bred illuminati of Madrid affecting French sniffed
at Goya's absence of poise, his violations of decorum.
Your mother, your sisters, your aunt believing you
a born carnal psychopath, a lying slut, head full
of sick black clouds of vampires, witches, demons.
Salve regina , mater misirecordiae you sing in the choir
thinking *Virgin Mary please please deliver me from evil.*
As Sister Camellia conducts, the big black rosary
at her side clicks against itself, and her sleeves flap like bats.
Daddy his brown suit, slicked hair, his docile wife
and your brothers and sisters fill an entire pew.
The priest beams on his good parishioner, his happy brood.
Sister Camellia's black rosary clicks and clicks.
Take off your nightie. Click. Take off your panties. Click.

2.

You owe obedience to your father as we owe obedience
to our Father in heaven, explains Sister Camellia.
Pater noster qui est in caelis. If he hurts you it must be
because you are bad. How does he hurt you? You cannot say.
That is darkness. In Goya's paintings how the subjects shine
amidst a great savage darkness that wants to crush them.
El Sueno de la razon produce monstrous. The sleep of reason yields.

Daddy. Looking at the family of the Duke of Osuna
you wonder which of the four is the dump child. You see fear
in the eyes of the small girl holding her daddy's hand.
And you are swallowed by another nightmare. Daddy holding
your hands, his friends on top of you, their whiskey breath,
their raspy cheeks rubbing yours. You want an axe to kill with.
To wield as the Spanish partisan in *Los Mismo*
over the French soldier himself writhing on a foe
like a man on his lover. Goya etching your soul.

Sister Camellia, is that you hooded and fleeing
beneath the witches feasting on someone in the air?
The black distended air whirling and whelping demons.
What penised menace nests in the Countess Chinchon
meek and misty in her bulging white sprigged muslin?
The philanderer Manuel Gody macho in military garb,
his thighs in palomino breeches, his walking stick
hanging suggestively between. The swinishness of men.
Even Jovellanos in his gleam of sweet reason
leaning on the ornate desk in the palace of Carlos
seems melancholy beneath the anvil of the night.

3.

The small *Caprichos* etchings tell still more of evil –
whores sweeping syphilitic customers, seen as roosters
plucked featherless, from their brothel. And the artist
sleeping while bats and owls flap about his head,
evil seeking a roost while reason dreams.
Panels from the walls of purgatory.
So much evil Ruskin set them on fire.
So much evil Sister Camellia would not look at them.
Your mother would say they are not what life is like.
And your father, would he recognize his heart?

In these images you can tell Goya wanted everyone free.
Yes, you as well. Freer than doctors and lovers have made you.
Or the absolutions that bound you to submission.
Free as Goya painting blithely in France before his death,
ideals destroyed, deaf, feeble yet captured by, capturing
the pure grace and beauty of a milkmaid in Bordeaux.

For you an abandoned church in which to paint and write
your life into peace. To make something of the sewage
and the pain. To be as clean and free as you have dreamed.
To return from the art, the darkness, your own
Arrieta, knowing as he did that *no hai remedio* –
no foot crushes all the writhing demons.
It is enough to create a cave of light.
A place to hold at bay the looming dark.

MIAMI HOLIDAY

Behind hotels flavoured peach and orange and lime
the breezeless shore features only two pelicans
feeding in the shallows by the pier and a few
inclined umbrellas barely concealing lovers.
The evening air is wetter than any the boy has breathed.
At last, he spies a phone booth for calling home
and telling the folks he's arrived okay. He wants to joke
about the snow up there which is what he is doing
when the pistol barrel is jammed against his throat.
Mom asking, "What did you say, dear? I didn't hear,"
while the boy with the pistol snarls, "Money. All of it."
He says, "Just a minute," annoying the pistol boy who
needs to please his mocking pals and score some crack
real quick, so he pulls the trigger. They split
back to the boulevard leaving the receiver dangling
over the sand where the dead boy lies bleeding.
Above him, a voice is repeating his name
over and over, the question mark becoming a screech,
which the closest pelican acknowledges,
turning, fish in beak, and blinking at the beach.

THE DOCTOR

No more boxers for me.
I'm a neurosurgeon
not a bloody botanist.

Tavern brawlers
that's another story.
They don't train
to destroy people.
No one pays to watch
a couple of drunks
smash furniture.

Four and a half hours
inside this kid's head
and *I'll* fight anyone
who calls it *sport*.

Nothing *technical*
about this knockout.
You want technical?
Bifrontal craniotomy,
three subdural hematomas,
possible embolisms,
possible skull fracture,
total left hemiplegia.

Let me translate.
If he ever wakes up:
half-life in the cabbage patch,
maybe complete loss
of his whole left side,
years of physio
so he can shuffle,
drool and gawk about.

No more boxers for me.
I'm not a bloody botanist.

VERN

I wuz okay once   Arnie sez.
Sometimes things   things kinda come
outa nowhere
        like a robe
silver robe
        blue words onna back
an then it's, y'know, gone.
Sometimes I can feel it
here...an here on my shoulders
feel it...sorta cool
here an smooth, y'know.

The gym has these pictures –
Arnie liftin up my hand
stuff outa newspapers...
newspapers...an they say
I wuz good once.

Arnie...he's good
a pal. He let's me do things
when no guys are there –
punch onea the bags or...
or, y'know, dance kinda
inna ring   sorta fightin
an I don't haveta pay
or clean up
        or pay money...

He claps, Arnie
when I do good things.
Jus him clappin
alone in the gym.
When he claps I...
is when I feel the robe...

So who knows he sez
maybe you'll come back
an I sez *from where*
an we always laff.

SPORTS ILLUSTRATED PHOTO

Black and white. Late afternoon. Staged. The sun, weak with winter, is in a haze behind the man, but his shadow topples like a victim to his right. The tracks must have been shuffled through the snow, not one distinct. They stop in mid-pasture, the snow beyond, broken only by a few frozen stems of weeds, sweeps into a black stretch of barren trees. The easy wind sifts like distant applause. Before the trees, a four-rail fence. No ropes now for Muhammad Ali in this larger ring, puffy-cheeked, alone on his farm in scarf and overcoat, coached by a photographer, squinting cloudy-eyed into lights. The tremors of his illness stilled by the quick shutter. The old gang who used to make and share the glory, gone – flung from Vegas to Maine, rummy rags and death to other vestibules of fame. Fabulous times, even when the reflexes flagged and the fists were pumped with novocaine. Even when the beatings began. Toasted by kings and presidents, entire floors in swanky hotels, the best of the best blazing fifteen years. Now all the colour is in the barn where he keeps framed photos and paintings of the bright-eyed bee and butterfly days. The glitzy robes, the entourage in jewels, the gorgeous wives. Showing the pictures to the visitor, he notices in nearly every one his almost pretty face is streaked with pigeon shit. Slowly he turns them to the wall. One by one. He walks outdoors. Into black and white.

HUDSON RIVER BREEZES
– Sept. 14, 2001

The breezes noticed first and told the birds.
For days updrafts pitched them left and right.
After the soot and dust had dispersed
people marvelled how morning
                    filled West Street,
its pavement and doorways ashen in the sun,
and spilled out onto the river, looking
uncertain without its matching stripes.
                  Breezes
piped the moaning of a woman in Battery Park,
her voice wavering but holding like a flag.

Now their onshore nudging teases Broadway
and ruffles Fulton Market unimpeded.
                      But
still, something is there. Now the shadow
of a great noise hangs in the air, as if an echo
of concrete and steel were welded to the sky.

HEROES IN COFFINS

Down fell the bold ones, too many, too often
Till not one was left and no one to implore.
There'll be no more kissing of heroes in coffins.

Imbued with belief, blind to all caution,
Advancing a cause in their fictions of war,
Down fell the bold ones, too many, too often.

Take down the pictures of flags held aloft in
A struggle the orphans refuse to explore.
There'll be no more kissing of heroes in coffins.

Most of them nameless, a few not forgotten,
Those some admired and chose to adore.
Down fell the bold ones, too many, too often.

Open the portals, let clean breezes waft in.
Their lethal impatience no longer ignore.
There'll be no more kissing of heroes in coffins.

Causes turn cancerous, integrity softens.
Righteousness burned, no flame can restore.
Down fell the bold ones, too many, too often.
There'll be no more kissing of heroes in coffins.

BORDEN AND MORRIS IN 2104

But it was daylight.
In the boughs of trees
space hung about like washing.
Through the snow
faces went by like flags before a fear.
— P. K. Page, "Failure at Tea"

The veranda where they sat
wore a membrane of factory soot.
Someone making something yet.
Misshapen owls began to hoot
But it was daylight

smeared with ash and dust
enough to smudge the sun
and stain the dwarfed and twisted buds
that drooped but clung
in the boughs of trees.

"Is that snow or smog?" Morris said.
"Same thing," replied Borden.
The syllables dropped and spread
as if oracular, words in
space hung about like washing

on a line. And soon a grey downfall
was slanting in a fretful breeze.
They could hear the compost ravens call
like waves of wounded infantries
through the snow.

Still people worried up the broken streets
and wild dogs foraged on the strand.
While Borden and Morris lapsed to sleep
sirens arced into the night and
faces went by like flags before a fear.

VORTAL TOMB, POULNABRONE, IRELAND

1.
Brink of day and nothing green
this side the burren in County Clare
near Galway, the sun flaring
south and east, rocks jutting
from heaves of limestone.

Later tourists will come to shoot
the tombs and utter comparisons
to the face of the moon.
                              Now it is me
and the almost sun and the tombs
filling with the thick caramel light.

O it's a haunted place they warned
some return nevermore themselves.

I give myself to that, not the fool.
The one with nothing green inside.

2.
Covert beauty in these barrens.
Gold moss robust on grey facets.
Symmetrical shadows of furrows
down rock faces. Limestone histories.
Chalky excrescence on the shady
sides of stones. The sky bronze
and orange and umber. Huge
slabs of the dolman in silhouette.

The absence of excess. Marvels
of the dim and the dull. Arid profusion.

I have no guide, no text to explain
the glaciation, the Karst drainage
system. I decipher memories
of absences and pungent emptiness.

3.
From stone we grind our lives.
Four thousand Christless years
of hunting and rituals and burials
and fifteen hundred more beneath
the priestly ways of Rome mean nothing
on these gaping wastes.
Lichen pale grey. Runnels on rock.

Who was he, hero of the raths,
whose axe made meat of flesh
and splintered bone?

        Who was she
he met behind the great heaved
stones? Wraiths on this wind.

    Whispering.

4.
Windalong voices.

         Place of death.

Gust smitten.

         Words of wrath.

Air in a rush.

         Cursed of Da.

Ears in a thrash.

         Da's red eyes.

Nothing bends.

         Ashes of rage.

When we set our slings aside
these stones will fly.
When we stop our killing
death will die.

5.
The wind rattles my jacket.
It slaps my chest and arms. That lone
noise like a flag's call to combat.
Fright in the blood. A short hike from the slow
green silence beneath the sea.

East of here a farmer's tractor split
the capstone of a buried cist
and opened to the sky a grave
filled three thousand years before.

With a rush the spirit swooped
out and gusts across this land
forever seeking haven. As we, soon
to follow, search each day. This memory
wind-implanted while the sun fumes.

6.
A place can own you.
Alone with the nameless dead
I drift out of today
towards their graves
yet away from fear.

Surrendering
I feel unbound.
Freedom is a union, not
unfettering. It is another way
the earth can have you.
Sublime submission.

It is the way of making things.
Stepping outside to be within again.
What unbinds ensnares.

7.
Six miles from the closest cottage,
I turn my back to the rocks
and there are more. But I gain
an angle on the wind. Its attack
flattens jacket and slacks
against my body. On the other
side they bulge and flap.

A land grey-brown and bleak,
rain-leached, vast – the burren.
Another country's wasteland
familiar as my nightly dream.
I've been here many times –
the desolate stretches, the wind's
lonesome blast. Home.

8.
A taffy sky with three white swans
winging to the sea. No place for hangings,
drownings, burials. They found ways,
to kill, ways to dump the dead.

When the seasons allow, in fissures
filled with meagre soil, grow rare
mountain avens, orchids, maidenhair.

Near what I think is the path back
a sinkhole and on its edge a fringe
of grass so sparse it has no shadow.

You will take the haunted burren
with you, the image-laden wind,
the wailings of gods forsaken.
And they will take you to your end.

THE GREEN BOOK

FIRST POEM

It is when the wind dies that he awakes
and sees the moon's blue gleaming
tinge the snow that now obscures the fences.
The street is like a chalice
rim to rim unmarred by feet or wheels,
a drink the storm has poured for him.
No time for socks, no time for shirt or mitts
or toque, just boots and pants and open coat
then out the door.
                So still, so white and cold.
He stops to let his eyes and lungs adjust
then plunges for the deepest drift, arms spread
and dives face first into its crest.
Boots and sleeves jammed with snow, he turns,
rushes back inside and runs upstairs
to view his imprint on the world.

THE GREEN BOOK

He writes things in a green book:
the dryness of an old bun
he has begun to eat,
morning's sun-blazed hills
across a prairie lake,
the pouch of stones pegged
beneath his stomach.
He is a poet. It is vital.

He pillages the green book:
the spray of flowers crushed
in a poet's dead eyes,
ashes filling the footprints
of an orphan on fire,
a German camera with a pistol
stalking a Texas street.
Minerals to mint into coins.

Coins to spend on editors:
the grey crust of semen
on his pant leg,
the red haversack
lumpy with unwashed socks,
a silhouette
of knotted flamingo necks.
Pounded. Polished. Pursed.

Editors test them with false teeth:
"sacred as brass cuspidors"
"the champagne and cellophane"
"brumous stuff of halos"
"the flexion of convention"
"an instant if camera-caught"
Dentists make good editors.

Your coins seem quite sound, but...
Roast beef on Ash Wednesday
is really too obvious;
Basque terrorists would not
bastinado in waltz time;
since you shot your lover
strangling is superfluous.
Lawyers make good editors.

He empties his green purse.
He is Laertes, a failure
on Ithaca, at Elsinore.
His tears turn to metaphors
and evaporate at dawn.
He prefers to love by proxy
and escape on pyrrhic feet.
He is a poet. It is vital.

FATHER TONGUE

Our language you say
is perverse and more
than metaphorically
masculine.

A linear grammar of pens
full of stallions,
testicles distended,
hooves stomping.

The daughters of the land
are offended, furious.
The beasts are not
Lipizzaners, will not

suffer braided reins or
flank-raking traces,
will not leave slopping
in their fetid wastes

to prance intricate
designs in rings;
favour the farmer's
coarse and loutish lads.

But these broncos fling
sons who strut in stripes,
refuse to be saddled
for easy musical rides.

All riders end sprawled
in reeking muck, thrown
by the bucking syntax,
the ambiguity unbridled.

HOW'S YOUR LAY-UP?

He goes to the gym
alone, at night
to practice fakes
and fancy dribbles,
but he never shoots.

He jumps,
he pivots,
but he never shoots.

Night after night alone
for hours he sweats
for the game/this game
now...

He dazzles ahead,
clears the key,
sends you in,
and sets you up
so beautifully...

Look!
The ball is in your hands!

A SAFE AND EASY THING

Don't stop reading, Mildred.
There's no need to be afraid.
This is not a poem. Pretend
you can hear me speaking,
pretend I am in a small room
far away playing the music
pictures happy in your head.

See? You don't need to think.
The words are small and easy,
the lines are short, the print
large, like an advertisement.
Nothing will happen to you,
nothing to buy or believe or give,
like pudding, pudding on a spoon.

No one will ask what this means.
No one will care you've read it.
It is almost over and nothing
has happened. Not the sniff
of a mention of something odd,
nothing shifty, nothing fancy,
not one unpleasant anything.

You can be proud of yourself.
Should there be a power failure,
should the bubble puddings stop,
in the cough and shuffle silence
here's something nice you can say
to your friends who never read,
not even signs or recipes.

Once I read a whole page of words
that my husband set into chunks.
It was easy, really, very easy.
It was about itself and me
and I could forget it right away.
That's something to flaunt safely.
It's not as if you'd read a poem.

ROADSIDE CONTRACTION

North of Pueblo, Colorado, an old guy
was pacing on the shoulder beside his
Malibu. Being a slow-moving
Canadian poet, I pulled a caesura.
"Sestina?" I inquired. "Nope. Sonnet.
Overheated to sixteen lines and steaming."
"Want some fresh eyes?" He hands me a frayed pad.
Choppy, non-iambic piece about arid
souls in a land of dunes and cactus.
In ten minutes we've pried out a wily
redundancy and snugged up lines thirteen
and fourteen, and she's ready for the road.
We drove to Mugsy's Lounge in Pueblo
and spent the evening discussing Eliot.

THAT SMALL RAIN POEM

He sailed and I malingered, not sick at all, except for her,
and I'd stop by her place and we walked the craggy shores
and talked of him and the weeks gone, then the weeks left till
he'd come, and clasp her fast, and sting her face with his new beard.

And when he did and she ran half up the gangway for his kiss
and folks all laughed and cheered, I slipped off down the shore.
He was a good man and good for her and would give her ample
joy before he drowned, no help nor harm from me bestowed.

So I went to where a gust had snatched her poem for him
as she was showing me, the sheet plunging like a gull to the swells,
the place in sand and shells and lime where, scraped and winded,
I'd stopped it with my boot and waited till she came to read it sweet.

(My sea chest locked beneath my bed all full of song on song
of love to her. Not a line in any one as honest strong as hers.)

She wore the navy bonnet low upon her brow, her sea-green
eyes fine and bright beneath the brim, and spoke that very poem.
When I had my voice I dared propose the change: to put the bed
in the last line and him and his arms in the third line, and she

changed it then and there and gave it him on his return. But now,
walking the shore and reading it again, I like her way of it better.
More full of strain it is and burns me more with salt to hear
her call to Christ and crave her bed, and then to have him in her arms.

SMALL RAIN DECEIT

I lied. She never wrote a word of it.
I suppose I wished, then said, she did
because I wanted her. I remember

no other wanting. And there were walks
far up the shore but never once we two
alone. Him and her. Me in the hills above.

And the time I did not ship with him
I was in Portsmouth too sick to stagger
let alone chase down a wind-tossed poem.

He wrote it. His only ever poem he said.
We were becalmed a week from shore.
He brought it with a lantern to my watch.

He knew I made poems. I read it and wept
all down inside myself and gazed far out
to the sea-touched stars and called it good.

But it was not good. It was beautiful
beyond anything I'll ever write, so pure
yet washed with pain from missing her.

When at last we docked it was her gift,
and they were wed and his next ship was lost
and she had his child and fell to sickness.

And me fetching wood and water for her
until she wasted to her grave, in part
to settle for the times I'd wished him gone,

the lies I told up and down, and because
I'd come to love her in a way free of fever.
And that's the all and final truth of it.

THE OLD SONG
for Patrick Lane

Nowlan dead.
His namesake
a grey cat
pads your rooms
a memory.

You say   unreel
time   stalk the past
see a response
leap

                              to the line

                  break

through   escape

and

                                                      flash!

That spasm past
that thrashing you say
listen to the rest

                  snowfall
                  on the dark lake

                  a branch
                  curved with oranges.

By the shore
we listen
and see

                  a toad
                  silvered with song.

SHE CLAIMS THE SKY

She sings the land out of winter, spring birth
and autumn death, none of them an end.
The undeflected winds that sweep sky to earth
and cease only to sigh and having sighed
gather and descend again, leaving trees,
shrubs and grasses seasoned, leaning east,
to these, she is an instrument long tried
that plays them as a breeze plays the seas.

Rosehips, leaves and seeds so slight they wedge
in the paw print of a fox. The print, its edge
faint in the dried mud of a marsh that shakes
with frogs and warblers ruffling the sedge –
all take substance from her voice the way light
is shaped by shadows and dust that breaks
it into colours. Also the refrains she makes
when she bathes in the wind-tumbled night.

When she bathes in the freckling day, the sun
soft on her skin, starts to bloom in her mind,
accepting that singular attention,
something isolate her solitude will refine
into a voice whose lyrics will sound
like us exalted. We will listen and surmise
it is artless artifice, something she found
on the wind and changed for us to recognize.

Never an end of fox prints, snow and spring,
us bending to them like sunflower stalks
ripe with the weight of her imagining.
Lichen bright orange on buffalo rocks,
wolf willow crowding a creek, horizons
of fossils beneath the horizon she claims,
and the vaulting sky besides, for the songs
of their living, the measure of their names.

ANGEL BEES
In memory of Anne Szumigalski

That spring in the land that looked flat but wasn't it rained every day. Water ran into the pores of the land and broke out in spontaneous ponds, and these merged into great shallow lakes so that there was no field where the sun couldn't see itself. Goaded by farmers' prayers for it to stay, the sun grew more vain than usual, lingered over these lakes and sipped so thirstily that the evening skies were piled with mountains of clouds. At night as everyone dreamed of oceans the clouds wept down onto the land, deepening and widening the lakes, which were fringed with more lilies than anyone could remember since the coronation of the ancient Harvest Queen.

Lily blossoms brought bees. In the homes of poets, velvet-bodied bees the size of hummingbirds appeared, one per dwelling as if assigned. Frightened, some poets opened doors and windows and chased them outdoors. Others smacked them with manuscripts. A few caught them and kept them in sealers and played with them until they died.

But the wiser ones knew better and left the bees alone, learned to live with the fat shadows that passed over their pages when the bees, eager for lilies, buffed their snouts on the windows. These poets became accustomed to the drone of the glassy wings, which was louder than the hum of the vacuum cleaners growing dusty in their unopened closets, as they wrote in a delirium such as they had never enjoyed.

Of course, in time the bees stung them. But painlessly, while they slept. And when they awoke the bees were gone and nowhere on the poets' bodies could one see a stinger-centred knot. Only later when the poets died and were examined was a strange node found on that part of their brains where words are sorted in honeycomb cells.

LAMENT FOR PURDY

From shining cod to shining salmon,
caribou to cow, the "Products of Canada"
map in those high school atlases
needs revision. In all regions among
tiny mines, lumber mills, fish plants,
grain elevators, add a poet at desk,
hair rampant, grasping a pen that sheds
a tumble of pages, on each a mini
map of Canada. Today the country
is Al Purdy's and all its people.
If he'd lived long enough, we'd all
have a line or two, even the weasel
politicians he cursed over beer,
even the sell-outs who don't know
they live in Eden and speed
its destruction, as if they could, as if
he would let us let them. And those
from whom we look away, especially
the ones who cling to the eaves.
This guy who couldn't pirouette if God
were the choreographer and recoiled
at corny lines, including his own, loved
graciously those the rest of us failed.
Also those he turned and gazed so long upon
back to our origins and beyond because
his mind didn't stop for death or birth,
the whole delightful planet needing to be loved.
The heedless dead he would lament
and bless with gruff praise, finding grace
in gutters as easily as St. Augustine,
finding in the flicker of his own pulse
God or a close relative and amidst
April daffodils the drums of death.
He recalled going naked in the snow
and dreamed white plumage to ride
over time unseen but not
                    unknown.

THREE THINGS WERE CERTAIN
in memory of Gwendolyn MacEwen

It was the Victory Theatre.
I think it was the Victory Theatre.
An old Toronto movie house.
Or perhaps burlesque.
It was 1970 I think
or 1971.

My first poetry reading
or one of my first
so I sat in the back row
or thereabouts,
two hundred people
between me and the stage.
Maybe 300.

In her long gold or saffron gown,
straight hair falling
or curled and twining
like shadows to her breasts
she seemed a priestess.
Or, against the black curtain,
a candle burning
in a window.

Clasping a book she never opened
she spoke magic for an hour.
It might have been longer.
Honey-brook voice.
Amber syllables.
I sat as if strapped in my seat, I
never leaned back.
I think it was red velvet.
It *was* red velvet.

TOWARD THE RIVER
for Henry

No wife, no cops to catch you
squeaking through winter bluster,
the river waiting patient as a postal box,
fish locked like stiff phrases,

& knowing it hits you hardest
in January, all that mass solid
down to the earth's eight ball core,
your blood a trickle freezing
on one of the words for snow.

Or it's another rehearsal & you return
tenured to plan tomorrow's classes –
the daily attrition by ignorance,
the daily cowardice by brilliance,
the protective glitter flaming
to ash in the old ash pan.

But no you've done it. The bridge
receding into clouds, your sleeves
applauding in the uprush breeze,
a grey bundle plummeting,
head cooling at last.
Filling at last
with words.

AIR FOR ONE JUST FALLEN
In Memory of John Hicks, spring 1999

Now it begins like rivers
in a far country where
a rootless tree
takes stout hold of air
with winter limbs alive
from the stored silence
of sun deep inside.
It only seems to sleep,
the season's simulation.

First, reeds with wind
in those high limbs
then grace of viols
and a slow dance
out of silence
into space.

The theme assumed
in rounded vowels
curled green
that slide into mind
before the eyes are through
with melodies of light.

And am I flagrant
in borrowed garb
shaped for bones
more elegant or
a ransacker
amuck inside
your house
disturbing dust on
fastidious lines,
distressing a mouse
about his work?

No matter. Art
never made substance
of sentiment
without a flaw
in the dance.

Except perhaps
in your new
circumstance.

THE FLUTE

Neruda said when he was alone
winter or a river shoved
poetry into his brain. Blind,
dumbstruck, on a lone wing, he
soared into the mind of the universe.
Poetry germinates in earth
and sea and sky. It rises
to grace those who listen in solitude.

It slides through language
like a goldeye and enters the world.
Too many glass-eyed scholars believe
poetry fills books the way gold
bars glint in vaults – aligned, neat,
negotiable. While they calibrate,
poetry, unheeded, circles outside,
gnaws through their power lines.

These things we call our selves
are metaphors of the universe
as natural as willow leaves,
ocean waves, volcanic vapours,
as natural as stones and beetles,
shapes of the presence that informs
all things and is all things, our myth
that we and they are separate.

Lines slip from calipers, slither
through the sides of vials, boggle
logarithms. When the presence
inside all things muses on beauty
wheat fields gleam in morning light,
corals secrete honeycombed cells,
Theta Orionis whelps a star
and the poet plays his flute of truth.

EVENI𝖭G LAUNCH

LAST QUARTER MAN

The shingles on his roof he swore
    were immune to moonlight.
Rainfall made them gleam
    a dark sheen in the dark night.

The porch sagged in the middle
    like an unhappy brow.
Rain flowed there and streamed
    down on the drooping steps

soaking no one. No one came.
    Weeds leaned onto the porch
as if to sip. In snowtime,
    one set of footsteps to and fro.

So dense so close were the trees
    that looking from his window
summer or winter his was
    the only image to be seen.

Music stayed out in the woods
    and ravines, wild grass blades
humming, and harmonies
    of finches, bees and leaves.

Inside, absence of moon and sun.
    Footsteps in rooms. The air
thin with things unspoken
    by the slim last quarter man.

THROATS OF STONE
Great archaeologists, like great artists, have curious minds
and intense imaginations. – Richard Leakey

To note what isn't there. To arrange
creatures in air the way once they
might have been and dream a tree
to hold them. One so real colleagues
calibrate its limbs. The best scientists
are poets who draw with metaphors.
Such as Salomon Reinach's leap
from the modern hunting totems of
Australian aboriginals to the cave
drawings of paleolithic people.

Hunting magic seemed a good theory,
and many archaeologists enjoyed
its shade. André Leroi-Gourhan
could not. He wondered why the beasts
on the walls were not the ones whose
bones fringed the ancient fire sites.
Why draw entrees not on the menu?
Maybe, thought Leroi-Gourhan, we have
discovered art and not a shopping list.
Caves of passions, visions, fictions.

He saw certain animals always put
in the same places in repeated patterns:
deer at entrances; oxen, horse, bison
in main chambers; tigers and panthers
snarling in the deep and narrow dark.
Other scientists concurred until sex
entered the pictures: Leroi-Gourhan
declared some images were male;
others, female. Gender wars ensued
and chainsawed the budding proposition.

Lately near Ariége two archaeologists
have been singing in the caves.
From tapes of their three octave span,
they drew graphs and maps of their music
and found the animal images massed
in places of highest resonance. Perhaps
shamans used these places to praise
and curse, echoes of shaking syllables
astonishing the select, spilling from mouth
of rock to sky. The earth in ecstasy.

In the flicker of voice and lamplight
off damp walls, and black clutches
of demons twitching left and right, tigers
may have prowled; panthers, lunged.
While glacial gusts howled above,
artists sang and made signs for music
in the long stone throats. Said: here
is magic, here our drums and whistles,
our voices will shake into meaning, will
reveal who sings these beasts and why.

A BRIEF HISTORY OF ZERO

1.
Before zero, holes in skulls,
mouths of caves did not
add up. There were spaces
we could not scale, murders
more than we could number.

Like eggs in the sands of India,
zeros waited to emerge –
disciplined citizens
in strict formations
for market calculations.

2.
From Babylon the Greeks
wrested a caravan of mere
plunder. The real wealth was
zero rattling like a golden egg
in one playful brain.

Its flawless arms held nothing
perfectly. It surged beyond one,
crushed old scores and ledgers
and sculpted infinity –
the orbits of planets and stars.

3.
Mad prophets saw it at the bottom
of sacred wells. Bid disciples
cast off sinful earth, destroy
their herds, kill enemies
and themselves in joy.

Zero where a village thrived,
and where the crops had waved.
Zero where the huts were razed,
zero in the cradles
and in survivors' eyes.

Adding zeros Hitler foresaw
the precise future of the Jews,
a solution in tall and tidy rows.
His skull still dreams blue-eyed
boys goose-stepping under halos.

4.
Zero on/zero off yields
complex computer codes,
remote nuclear devices, digital
intimacies, the age of space,
and voice-activated toilets.

Zero's what the earth will total
in not so many zeros aligned
behind an unrelenting one –
a perfectly oxidized disc
rapidly spinning nowhere.

NOVEMBER

Brittle leaves scuttering the street.
        Streams of chimney smoke blurring into clouds.
Wind grey and sleek packing gutters with snow.
        Trees bleak, beyond meaning now,
not manic cuneiform, not gestures of disease,
        not eunuchs grim in the shrill light.

You lean to these. You feel knees spreading to release you.
        Hands that clasp and knot
your bleeding. You feel your breathing begin,
        the vague pain fibrous beneath
your scream. You see the grey radiance, the white spaces,
        the sheen of polished steel.

You feel the topaz talisman. Its pale gleam.
        You receive drawings of a beast, a sky,
so that you may see all that you are, all that you will be.
        An amber fog twines along
the water where you must kneel, the river that meanders
        deep into the hallowed land.

The river becomes a creek freezing. A forgotten tent torn,
        dreaming of grass, dreaming
of arms, lovers humming. Shreds filling with distance
        and the wreckage of reeds.
The hermit of the sedge who would have hailed you
        has retreated to another month.

Sleep is your response. Sleep defeats time.
        Until something in you stretches, yawns
and conceives spring, even now, and you clamber the slopes
        steeper and steeper
to celebrate winter's easing. The air cuts deep.
        You breathe keen flakes of glass.

No thaw. The month moves with you, your cowl.
The moon a gleam on the creek's
dark ice. Something wants warmth, something sings fire.
You gather willow splinters,
the stems of rushes, leaning stalks of yellow grass.
You will please whatever sings.

A THIN PLACE

Beneath the mute cross,
rows of pews trap light, drop
shadows in the vacant church.

Doubt and I share a pew.
His mocking brings me here,
faith kept safe from excess.

We try to stay our course,
in this thin place between heaven
and hell, beneath a capsized keel.

He gives me freedom to not
believe, to strive with his great
brawn and, if I wish, to yield.

God's peace is no peace at all.
Doubt sees to that while I stay
naive with dreams and even

dance to tease the demons. I
fret myself to sleep, and each
day learn to breathe again.

PRACTICE OF GREAT HARMONY

Your bones are not a rig to hoist you from
the earth, your muscles not cords to lug you
up. Let gravity have its weigh; fall numb
into your centre, melt into your feet through
softness, limbs loose, as a tiger might stalk.
Feel small birds lifting from your head. They rise
in heat and light. Wear the yang gaze of hawk
about to strike and then the yin of dove's eyes.
Move while rooted. Walk as a tree might walk,
directed by the trunk, to where light draws.
A tree that seeks the image of a long
intent, without stutter, without pause.
Be like the tree that thinks leaf and moves because
it hears inside itself a slow green song.

AT THE LAST SERMON OF THE 14th DALAI LAMA

It is raining and O the rain is singing
on my skin like happy children
spawned in clouds that skid on snow
in the great Kashmiri mountains.

Rain amidst the monasteries
will wash away the small of faith
sweep them into tents to shiver
broken incantations.

Be silent, be still, O my brothers.
Seek to trace the sacred stair
the Buddha spins for us
with the sermon of The Wheel of Time

we climb through skyface
into *sunyata*
beyond even the smell of things
incense and butter-oil,
earth wetness, soaked hair
above our bodies in the square

(now the singing ceases
flesh   ceases
beards/lips
dissolve

rain flavour
is all of me

i am
a single   syllable
as   words
          un
                link
                     them
                          selves

                                        O

REFLECTIONS: THE LOVE OF MIRRORS

They say the mirror in Elvis Presley's bathroom
never forgot him, that men looking in
see a piece of Elvis looking back. They say
Dali painted a nude self-portrait on the wall
opposite his so it would not be lonely,
and that years after Peter Sellers died
his could be heard doing impersonations
in accents at night. The day Indira Gandhi
was slain tears dribbled down her glass.
In Frida Kahlo's: a v of crow's wings.

In the way of mirrors, yours watches you try
expressions, check your tongue, your degrees
of modesty. It sees your blemishes, your secrets
and never whispers them. As you settle down
your mirror accepts those deepening lines,
the thinner greying hair, the sagging parts.
It does not pretend, compare, resist the light.
No one ever loves you like your mirror, not
your lover, nor your mother, not even you
in any of the versions trapped in its layers.

The time will come when you will not be
in your mirror. Patiently the glass will wait
for you to wash and brush your teeth,
for the graze of your self-regarding eyes,
but you will not appear. Each day it will retain
less and less in the silver cells of its memory.
And soon someone new will stand before it
and the mirror, charmed by a leaner body
that requires less reflective energy, will try
again to find a lustre thin enough for myth.

EVENING LAUNCH

Alone, just him and the shadowing lake and the sun
spreading the day's last benediction on the hills.
No thought of her, he crouches on the stone-thick shore,
his boat lifting to scrape a jagged spur by his knee
and falling back again and lifting, like a patient grief.
Between his hands he holds the last of what he has to load,
pages that had burned under his eyes in lantern light
and then burned again inside of him. Turning to dust.
He wedges them in among the other things that failed
and sits a long time on his heels, silent, waiting to learn
what is next, surprised he feels no urgency to know.
Then come the words, slow, mumbled in the same
low key as the grinding hull, stumbling out of him
like old men who sleep too long and wake in pain.
It seems that they are something like a prayer
though to whom and for what is unclear.
He has never heard his voice so gruff and hushed,
so unyoked and unconcerned with what it might achieve.
Wrapping the tether rope around his hand
each loop neater and larger, he places the mane
of long white threads to his lips, the nuzzle
in his words. He slips his hand free and holds
a tapered nest of coils. As the light subsides
he whispers his last words into this dark bowl,
his lips brushing rough braid, then he tosses it
onto the load, reaches down, cups the prow
and thrusts the boat out into the lake. He stands
and watches it glide, catch a current and swerve
as if it has a sense of where it has to go.

LATENESS

It's never as late as you think.
It's always later.

You have two preschoolers,
you go to a movie, come home,
a phone call from Paris –
the youngest on her honeymoon.

Those countless times you speak or kiss
too late.

The dog who disappears in mid-bark.

Your father and mother wave
from their last car and never return
leaving a tangle of lost
intentions.

Drifts of words in your head,
waiting for the right stage,
the right page, yesterday's
replays.

Your mind not recognizing
your body.

The mechanism that lets us think
it's not too late keeps us alive
until it is.

STAKES IN THE RIVER
A day of rotations, after James Richardson

1.
Time stolen is the best time.

2.
Holding on to afternoons is the hardest holding.

3.
Staying home, the most demanding journey.

4.
Time begrudged, the saddest time.

5.
Time accelerates travel.

6.
Despair says I cannot do it all. Joy says I cannot do it all.

7.
Love and time are one.

8.
Distance becomes time; nibbles love.

9.
For a time you sat on God's lap. When was that?

10.
Genius is giving others the kind of time they need.

11.
I cannot touch you without touching time.

12.
You confess to squandering time to validate your potential.

13.
A still night – stones fall from the wall of memory.

14.
Drudgery degrades time.

15.
A wound that does not heal over time is not a wound – it is you.

16.
How fast from *adore* to *abhor*?

17.
Time heals as snow heals – one colour that blurs and blunts.

18.
They give most who give time.

19.
The writer craves your time. You crave...?

20.
Try not to hear what is not said before it is not said.

21.
Seeking to comprehend time is time lost.

22.
Art undoes time. A stake in the river.

23.
The last interruption forestalls all others.

24.
In the end, enough time has elapsed since the start.

LEARNING TIME

You get an overdose at first, before
you know what it's worth. So long,
so long, you lie there drooling
and lumping your diapers until
you're set on the floor where you
crawl and wobble like time
itself. And then the bell for school
where you learn to tell and bide.

Numbered, time accelerates
and manages never to be where you
throw the ball. Always a week to Santa,
a month to summer vacation.
But some days stall the sun
as you emulate the plants –
not moving, not thinking, becoming one
with dirt, an obstacle for ants.

The flicker from Friday after school
to Monday's bell, the lag of the classroom
clock, its minute hand thinned by eyes
that urge its stuttering advance.
Then time of the boy, going from girls
to women, the hoped-for chance,
the shadows, the shadings, the long space
between no and never and yes and always.

Gaining patience imparting patience
to your children. The way you build
snowmen with ever smaller globes.
The stories when your sons snuggle
against you and end in slumber.
The hockey games with each period
shorter than the last. Did you sleep
too much away and rush conclusions?

You squeeze a mid-life crisis between
the knee operation and hip replacement.
And there you are – an arthritic apparatus
for grandchildren with seasons flying
off like the boy-next-door's pigeons
(his name a blur in the flurry) the time
he set them free. And then, and then
you're in bed, and it isn't long at all.

IT BEGINS WITH A

It begins with A.

                                          It does not end

with Z
but coils around it like a noose.

This is not possession,
The cancer is possession, a gang amok
inside my organs.

This is abandonment.

                                          My sons

leaving as I knew they had to but
mad at the old fool, the hometown.

I don't know what's gone. She hands me
paper, tells me I must write, shows
me a book with a picture of me

on the back when I was married to
the other one, tells me I wrote
the peculiar things inside.

So much seems pretense,
a game preferred
to people.

I write directions, steps
to pilot this machine, that routine.
But my lists think it's autumn.

And I cannot read his writing.

She retypes, repairs the blunders.

Most days she visits. Or do I?
Outside snow dithers
against walls, drops in piles.

There is a name for that.

This is not a ploy. It *is*
winter.

How can one be amazed by grey?
The ascension of feeble?

I cannot sleep like the others.

Again I am afraid of the dark.

I shovel snow at dawn.

If I succeed you will not believe me.

FROM ARGUMENTS IN THE GARDEN OF PRAYER

1.
So many frogs are extravagant with song
the sky is crammed. A calculation might
reveal at any given moment at least
twelve to be in natural harmony.

The meadowlark on the barbed wire
sings so I will look away from her nest
out to where the grass reaches my knees.

Here it is trimmed, exposing badger holes
snugged to the concrete cap across a grave.

Maybe twenty tombstones. Half of them my kin.

They carried her name before my mother,
unknown to her, those in this other place.

Easy to believe lives of peace and ease.
Beyond, in disagreement, wheat sags in the heat.

6.
Honour the land, honour God. Who is God
of this fire-blackened hollow? Not even
the ants have returned. A dried thistle rattles
by a black rock. That is all but for ash
on the wind. No bush. No trees. Burnt grass
bristle stiff and dusting underfoot.
A dismal scoop of hell. The place where Satan
laughed and scorched belief to the roots.
In the black midst, death on death, the skeleton
of a fox, white, delicate as scripture.
A language untranslatable now.
You know the code will be broken, meaning
teased into greenness. But today
you must walk away. You must leave it behind.

7.
Thick heat rides the high noon wind
that slams my face. My camel has six
cylinders and twenty-four loan payments.
I start the air conditioning. That's progress.

Because I'm not sweating on a gangly,
cud-spitting, farting beast and foraging
for rats, you exist. I am going forward
with Merton and Chardin in the back seat.

You ride with us because I need to believe
we are moving beyond camels and cars
and holy massacres to some transcendence.

In a blink the universe expanded
from a marble to every single thing.
That's when we think we heard your fingers snap.

10.
Each day is sunny and clear; each night, rain
that need not fall on farms, highways, cars.

This great plain awakening with April grass
needs nothing more than it already has

to be what it is, what it will be. The future
does not crave our hands, our words to name

its changes and sustainings. It will awake
when we do not awake.
                              There need not be

grain waving at clouds or cattle in corrals
for you to be. Whether we are amusement,

experiment or rudiment, we are not
able to know if you tend the meadow.

A sparrow begins a nest with blades of dead
grass. She will fill it with tomorrow.

11.
prayer is our way of making you
holy
    reverse creation

we cannot say if our pain
     this blade that scrapes
     inside our brains
is yours or not

either way nothing changes
but ourselves

the shaman walks in an early morning field

we observe, conclude
his sandals are drenched with dew

when will it stop
   this idiot making
   of cause and consequence

12.
Prayer is one way not to starve yourself
when you have a famine of the heart
or the future is cancelled, except for pain.
Pilgrim if you can. Blood on the forehead,
blood on the knees, shoulder gouged to bone
from a cross dragged up the prescribed
stone steps in wind, raw from the salty waves,
cutting and cold, to a holy place where
a relic is encased.
                    Or wait in covers
in your final bed, and change your life
as much among the comforts of your kin,
your fate no less as you twist upwards
on a stem of agony, shrunk and waxy
gray, belated love struggling in your throat.

13.
There is nothing here. What is this place?
Not even light. Not even you. Nor sound.

Not even the soothing hum of grace.
Agony squeezed you shut. Then this, this

opening. What is this absence you feel?
An oscillation of pain made bodiless?

You would like to remember something
for context or comparison, a grid

of logic for the nonexistent ground,
a sky you could cancel with your hand.

Nothing comes. You think this might be
the perfect space for divinity

to blaze into a rose you could love.
But is this you? Were those vapours words?

14.
The first sounds will be the bottle rattle
of the milkman and the chattering sparrows.
You don't get up right away. You listen
to your mother clatter in the kitchen,
your father shaking out the paper.

The endless sun spills through the window.
You think of school. All your homework is
ready and all correct. New clothes beckon
in the closet. A playground of friends awaits.

Your father's voice, low and casual,
spreads warmth and your mother's voice responds.
One of them turns on the radio.

A voice declares eternal peace and welcomes
you to heaven. Stretching, you decide to rise

AFTERWORD

Poetry entered me before I knew what it was. I thus had no defense against it, nor would I have wanted one. It has been my source of pleasure and consolation for over fifty-five years. Now that I have been diagnosed with a terminal illness, and my mobility becomes increasingly limited, it sings on – the words of others and words that might be my own. As my capacity to do other things diminishes, I want poetry to take a more central place than ever.

As a child of six I wanted to move people, preferably many at a time. I craved the ability to take people from here to there, and dreamed they would seek to experience my power. I imagined a uniform, as well. In short, I wanted to be a bus driver. By the time I was a teenager I wanted to move people with words and had had some very limited success. By then I was reading poetry widely and indiscriminately. I bought paperback translations of Homer for 60¢ and the selected works of Marvell, Donne, Coleridge, Blake, Browning, Keats, Shelley, Wordsworth and Dickinson, my earliest influences, among others, in Laurel Paperback editions for 35¢ each. Shakespeare's sonnets set me back 50¢. I have read these small volumes many times since then and still go back to them. Today, it is astonishing to realize that I bought these books at newsstands that displayed Mickey Spillane, Max Brand, and Grace Metalious. Would that poetry still had a place on bestseller shelves.

I also lingered often in the poetry section at the Moose Jaw Public library where I discovered and delighted in Dante, Yeats, Eliot, Frost, Auden and Wallace Stevens. Encountering poetry like theirs outside of any classroom was exciting to me, each book a challenge and journey. What was a muddle-headed sixteen-year-old Moose Javian to make of "The Idea of Order at Key West" or "The Wasteland"? I was responding to the voices, the bold forays in or against the traditional styles and the music. Whatever meaning seeped in I considered a bonus.

Not that I wasn't interested in the poetry we studied in St. Louis College, the Catholic boys' school I attended. In fact, I had one superb teacher of English literature in grades nine, eleven and twelve, Sister Ida Marie Grenon, who seemed to love every piece that she taught, and I certainly was receptive to that passion. I recall especially enjoying Shakespeare, Burns, Wordsworth, Browning, Shelley, Tennyson and Housman. Later, at university, I discovered and was influenced by other poets: Neruda, Robinson Jeffers, E. A. Robinson, Rilke and, almost as an afterthought, a few of my countrymen – F. R. Scott. A.M. Klein, Irving Layton, Leonard Cohen, Alden Nowlan, and John Newlove.

After completing high school, I worked a year as a labourer and then as an office clerk at the Canadian Pacific Railway in Moose Jaw. It was during that year of intense reading and writing that I got serious about poetry. My office duties included filing and duplicating. Upstairs from the office was the duplicating room and the archive file room, next to which was a storage closet of perhaps twenty square feet with possibly seven square feet not occupied by shelves. To this cell, I added a chair. Behind the stacks of paper, I secreted the book of poetry I was currently reading. I never lacked for paper, of course. My favourite writing tablets were the legal-sized, ruled pads popular with our executive secretaries. I would make every effort to get my work done so I could have some time in my nook, though never too long, perhaps twenty minute stretches before I would make an appearance at my desk, do something or other and then dash back upstairs. So I was a true closet poet and thus began a series of windowless writing and reading rooms where I would turn off the phone and devote myself to poetry with few distractions while ignoring time, weather, and deadlines. I would read or write for hours and emerge to find the outside world transformed by a deluge or blizzard.

All this time I was writing these early poems – mostly very derivative, awkward efforts in the manner of some of the poets I admired – I also did some boxing and played baseball, hockey and football. None of my classmates or teammates knew I was committing poetry. I would never have been able to tolerate the gibes. Such were my rogue teenage years. One member of the crowd I was part of went on to be a mechanical engineer who ended up teaching high school science and math. Later, after I had published five or six books, he'd have a few drinks and phone me well into the night. "Hyland, what is this shit you write? I can't understand it." He had read at least one of the books but claimed to have a mind completely antithetical to poetry. I tried, even in those circumstances, to convince him he could read and enjoy poetry.

I was in my mid-thirties with perhaps thirty poems published in various magazines before I felt comfortable calling myself a poet. About then, at the urging of my best friend Bob Currie, whom I regarded as a real poet, I joined a writing group which we eventually called The Moose Jaw Movement and which later evolved into The Poets' Combine. Monthly meetings of these groups kept me writing, gave me invaluable feedback and produced wonderful friendships, not to mention some performance opportunities and great social occasions. With a few exceptions, the poems in this collection were workshopped with those talented people between 1975 and 2007.

As I write this, I am looking at a book called *Poets' Choice*, purchased by mail order in 1963 when I would have been twenty-two. I remember how rapturous I was to receive it. I had long loved reading anthologies and this one, an all-star collection, edited by Paul Engle and Joseph Langland, asking the poets to select their favourite poems and supply a rationale for their selections, promised to be crammed with great poems. It was not. By that time I was conversant with much of Frost, Cummings, MacLeish, Berryman, Lowell, and Larkin, and thought their choices and those of most of the others did not represent their best. I see that I checked off as worth reading again only those of Patchen, Layton, Cohen, Shapiro, Birney, X. J. Kennedy and Ogden Nash. With these exceptions, it seemed to me the poets proved to be inept judges of their own best work.

My disappointment in that book and subsequent similar experiences led me to mistrust the idea that poets, including me, could be reliable judges of their own poetry. For this reason, when it was suggested I might assemble a volume of selected poems, I was both pleased and leery. I thought for some time about who might bring a discerning eye to the editing. One of the first names that came to mind is, in fact, the editor of this volume. Amy Caughlin had not only read but commented trenchantly on much of my poetry. I found her to be demanding and observant, so I was delighted when she agreed to edit this book.

I still devour poetry and continue to write it. I intend to do so until this illness I have (ALS or Lou Gehrig's disease) makes it impossible to carry on. And then, having lived life full tilt and loved it all enormously, I will be gone.

– Gary Hyland

INDEX OF SOURCES

NOTES ON SOME OF THE POEMS

The Dulls: The quotation is adapted from Shakespeare's *The Merchant of Venice*, V, i, 83–86.

Delusions: is based in part on the book *The Man Who Mistook His Wife for a Hat* by Oliver Sacks.

Yugen (Japanese): a feeling derived from the heightened perception of transient beauty so that one experiences a state of meditative enchantment and feels out of the flow of time.

White Crane Spreads Wings: is based on Japanese tales from *The Mystery of Things* by Patrik Le Nestour.

Hammel: All that is known of the imaginary character Aldred Hammel is from a partially-burned diary that survived a fire in which he incinerated his letters and manuscripts. Sociologist Wilhelm Kreuzer came into possession of the diary and decided to do an in-depth investigation of Hammel's life as part of his study of the contributing factors to the alienation and marginalization of underachieving North American males. Most of the details in the poems are from the diary, which covers the subject's last years from November 1998 to November 2003, a week before his death. Several of the entries contain recollections and reflections from his earlier days. He was born in Regina, Saskatchewan, Canada, in 1939, and, except for a year or two of college, spent most of his life there working as a file clerk for the British-American Oil Company, later Gulf Oil and presently Gulf Canada Resources.

Winter Moths: Thanks to Paula Patola and her Saskatoon English class who provided a stimulating assignment that led to this poem.

The Wild Yird-Swine: In the mythology of Scotland and England, the yird-swine or earth pig was a loathsome creature said to devour corpses. *Folklore of North-East Scotland*, Walter Gregor, 1881.

Mildly Manic: was inspired by Alex Beam's *Gracefully Insane*, a history of McLean Hospital, a mental institution just outside of Boston, that housed the likes of John Nash, Sylvia Plath and Robert Lowell.

Child Running: was inspired by Associated Press photographer Nick Ut's famous photo of eight-year-old Kim Phuc running naked along a road in Vietnam.

Lian, Lian: is based on a Nov. 15, 1989, AFP news story from Beijing.

Danica At The Goya Exhibition: is derived from *Don't: A Woman's Word* by Elly Danica, 1988, Gynergy Books.

Sports Illustrated Photo: was in the April 28, 1988, edition of the magazine.

Vortal Tomb, Poulnabrone, Ireland: The breathtaking burren south of Galway is named from a Gaelic word meaning stormy place. Unspoiled since the ice age, the vast area contains a collection of megalithic tombs with relics of humans dating back 6,000 years. The vortal (or entrance) tomb near Poulnabrone is the most famous of the dolmans. The area also has numerous earthen ring forts called raths.

That Small Rain Poem, and *Small Rain Deceit:* Originated in an animated exchange with Saskatoon professor and writer Ron Marken that involved speculation about the backstory to the exquisite sixteenth century poem reprinted below.
> *Western wind, when will thou blow,*
> *The small rain down can rain?*
> *Christ! if my love were in my arms,*
> *and I in my bed again!*

Last Quarter Man: Claiming the last homestead in a municipality in Saskatchewan usually meant acquiring land of inferior quality and the poorest quarter section of that was often where the claimant's home was built.

Throats Of Stone: is based on a portion of Richard Leakey's *The Origin of Humankind,* Basic Books, 1996.

A Brief History Of Zero: owes a debt to *Zero: The Biography of a Dangerous Idea,* Charles Seif, Penguin, 2000.

A Thin Place: was inspired by a piece by Nora Gallagher in a long-lost issue of *The Utne Reader.*

Practice Of Great Harmony: originated from the conjurations of Harold Hajime Naka, inspirational tai chi instructor.

At The Last Sermon Of The 14th Dalai Lama: This sermon, called The Sermon of the Wheel of Time, was delivered to an estimated 18,000 adherents during an icy downpour at Leh, India, in 1976. It is one of Buddhism's most elaborate rituals, an eight hour address on tantrism. The Dalai Lama explained that one of the requirements for the supreme level of tantric experience is a correct understanding of *sunyata* or nothingness. The Dalai Lama delivers this sermon a maximum of only six times during his lifetime. The 1976 presentation was the sixth sermon for the current Dalai Lama.

Stakes In The River: is derived from James Richardson's "Vectors: Forty-Five Aphorisms and Ten-Second Essays" that appeared in *Ploughshares* in 2000.

ACKNOWLEDGEMENTS

Some of these poems first appeared in the following publications: *Grain, Salt, Chelsea Annual, Sundog, Elfin Plot, CVII, Quarry, Fiddlehead, Canadian Forum, New Quarterly, Canadian Literature, Wot, Repository, Cross Canada Writers' Magazine, Wascana Review, NeWest Review, Pierian Spring, Capilano Review, Prism, Prairie Journal of Canadian Literature, Prairie Fire, Freefall, Windsor Review, River King Poetry Supplement, Event, The New Chief Tongue 3.* Some were broadcast on CBC Radio programs Basic Black, Anthology, Ambience, Gallery, and Between the Covers.

My gratitude to the Moose Jaw Movement and the Poets Combine for their insights and suggestions, in particular, to Byrna Barclay, Bob Currie, Judith Krause, Bruce Rice and Paul Wilson.

To Amy Caughlin, sincere thanks for the dedicated and discerning eye and the encouragement.

Thanks to Lorna Crozier for her friendship, inspiration and encouragement.

Without the loving devotion of Sharon Nichvalodoff this book would not have been completed.

ABOUT THE AUTHOR

Gary Hyland is a Saskatchewan writer, teacher, cultural activist, consultant and editor who has already published six full-length books of poetry and two chapbooks. He co-edited the humour anthologies *100% Cracked Wheat* and *200% Cracked Wheat* and the poetry collections *Number One Northern* and *A Sudden Radiance*. His work has appeared in numerous anthologies and journals both Canadian and international.

A finalist for the Milton Acorn People's Poet Award for *White Crane Spreads Wings*, Gary has also been short-listed for the National Magazine Gold Medal Poetry Award, and has received numerous other awards and prizes. He was named a Member of the Order of Canada in 2005. He resides in his birthplace of Moose Jaw, Saskatchewan, where he was named lifetime Poet Laureate (with Robert Currie) in 1991, and was twice declared Citizen of the Year. In 2007 he was named one of the 100 most influential graduates of the University of Saskatchewan in the last one hundred years.

See Gary's Web site for further details: *www.garyhyland.com*